KEN
RUSSELL

a guide to
references and resources

A
Reference
Publication
in
Film

Ronald Gottesman
Editor

KEN
RUSSELL

*a guide to
references and resources*

DIANE ROSENFELDT

G.K.HALL&CO.
70 LINCOLN STREET, BOSTON, MASS.

Library of Congress Cataloging in Publication Data
Rosenfeldt, Diane.
  Ken Russell

  (A Reference publication in film)
  Bibliography: p.
  Includes indexes.
  1. Russell, Ken, 1927-   I. Title.   II. Series.
PN1998.A3R777   791.43'0233'0924   78-1276
ISBN 0-8161-7881-X

This publication is printed on permanent/durable acid-free paper
MANUFACTURED IN THE UNITED STATES OF AMERICA

Contents

Preface

Notes on the compilation of this book:

Biographies: The biographical section is a synthesis of information culled from a number of articles and interviews. It relies heavily on John Baxter's book, An Appalling Talent, which contains extensive biographical information on Russell in his own words. Basic facts were extracted from the 1975 volume of Current Biography.

Synopses and credits: An asterisk (*) preceding an entry number in this section indicates that I have not seen the film and that my information is based on secondary sources. In these instances the synopsis was based on any available published synopses and, whenever possible, the original work upon which the film was based. When I was familiar with the film, I wrote from memory, checking myself, again, against published synopses and original works. Credits lists were culled from the most complete published lists available. For synopses and credits, Filmfacts and the British Film Institute's Monthly Film Bulletin were consistently helpful.

Bibliography: The entries in this section cover a time span beginning in 1964--when Russell started attracting notice--to October, 1977. The entries are as comprehensive as possible. I consulted every available film index, as well as other relevant indexes. I also searched through a voluminous amount of unindexed material. Research was done in: the Wyllie Library-Learning Center of the University of Wisconsin--Parkside; the Gilbert M. Simmons Library (both in Kenosha); and the Memorial Library of the University of Wisconsin--Madison. I also used some material from the University of Southern California.

The initials [BFI] in Monthly Film Bulletin entries stand for British Film Institute. The initials [NB] after an entry indicate that I found the newspaper article in News Bank, a microfiche system which reproduces articles and reviews from papers across the country. The articles are arranged by subject and printed in full except for page numbers and sometimes, unfortunately, by-lines. In such cases I have listed the entries as "Anonymous." Full bibliographical information for News Bank is as follows:

<u>News Bank Review of the Arts</u>:   <u>Film and Television</u>.

    1975:   Greenwich, Connecticut, 1975.
    1976:   Greenwich and Stamford, Connecticut, 1976.

Most underground newspaper entries are from the Underground Newspaper microfilm collection of Bell and Howell and the Underground Press Syndicate.   I found microfilm editions of newspapers and the several volumes of the <u>New York Times Film Reviews</u> to be very helpful.

Citations with an asterisk denote articles I have not personally seen.   For these I have noted my source for the citation in brackets after the entry.   In some cases the full bibliographical citations were too unwieldy to reproduce fully.   These appear below.

<u>British Humanities Index 1967</u>.   Edited by Betty M. Mason, A.L.A.
    London: The Library Association, 1968.
<u>British Humanities Index 1974</u>.   Edited by Betty M. King, A.L.A.
    London: The Library Association, 1975.
<u>International Index to Film Periodicals 1972</u>.   Edited by Karen
    Jones.   New York and London: R. R. Bowker Co., 1973.

In the case of foreign-language articles, I have tried to translate all but the most obvious titles.   I have not translated titles in languages unfamiliar to me.   Whenever possible I have based my annotations on my own rough translations; otherwise I have scanned the article for key words.

Acknowledgments: I would like to thank Ron Gottesman for his interest, guidance and friendship.   I am also grateful to my parents, Dorothy and Ralph, and to countless friends for enduring my monomania as I prepared this book; to Peggy Runge for divers invaluable aid; to the Story family, Alberta, Larry, Amy <u>et al</u>., for food and general moral support (not necessarily in that order); and to Antoinette Bloxdorf and Jockey International for unwittingly providing me with the time and resources to begin my researches.

Early Biographical Background

Ken Russell makes strange movies out of the lives of strange people. It is appropriate, then, that his own life, while not as bizarre as his subjects', has had its moments of high improbability.

Henry Kenneth Alfred Russell was born on 3 July 1927 in Southampton, England. His parents were thoroughly middle-class; the father had inherited the family shoe business. Ken was an only child until the age of five, and seldom played with other children, instead inventing his own amusements. His strongest memories of his early life were of family gatherings and almost daily teas and cinemas with his mother. Considering this cinema diet it is not surprising that by his tenth year Ken had his own small, hand-cranked projector and a collection of short films, mostly cartoons. As time went on, his equipment became more sophisticated. He ran some old, hand-tinted travelogues on an ancient 35 mm projector; he was fascinated by the effects made by the tinting. He got his first taste of artistic films when he found a drug store that rented films by Fritz Lang and Leni Riefenstahl.

Russell was sent to boarding school, where he discovered Betty Grable musicals and Warner Brothers films. He developed a crush on Dorothy Lamour and longed to sail to the South Seas. He thought his dream was coming true when he was fifteen and his father let him go to Pangbourne Nautical College, but he was in for a bad time. He was persecuted by the wealthier cadets for his middle-class clothes and accent. He found the place rigid and archaic, and was neither interested in, nor particularly apt at, seamanship. He lived for the weekends, when he would sneak into town to see movies, after which he would usually return to school and be punished.

Russell volunteered to produce the College's annual divisional concert, which had traditionally been boring and bad. His first production, featuring some of the cadets in drag and a lot of big-band jazz, was less bad and a good deal less boring. The authorities, however, were not amused.

It was here, at Pangbourne, that Russell made his first film --a sort of melodramatic slapstick horror story which disappeared after its first showing.

Russell graduated from nautical school and entered the Merchant Navy as Sixth Officer on a cargo ship bound for the Pacific. His South Seas dreams quickly died. He did not get along well with his eccentric captain or the crew and was chronically seasick. He almost jumped ship in Australia, until he realized that he didn't like Australia either.

Then the war ended, the cruise ended, and Russell's nautical career ended. His parents assumed that he would then join the family shoe business. Horrified at the thought, he tried to get into the film business, fruitlessly making the rounds of the studios with great zeal and no experience.

It was at about this time that Russell discovered classical music, in the form of Tchaikovsky's First Piano Concerto. Some people become fond of things and dabble; others become obsessed and plunge. Russell was the latter type. As he had earlier plunged into film fanaticism, so he now immersed himself in classical music, to the point of playing Stravinsky at full volume while bounding about the house in athletically performed nude interpretive dances.

Wishing to avoid the shoe store at all costs, Russell joined the Royal Air Force in 1946 and, after a bad session at a transit camp, signed up to be an electrician. However, at the electricians' training camp, he discovered that he was not suited to be an electrician. It was there that he met a sailor named Bert who also loved classical music, and together they ran the camp's Music Circle. Russell was astounded and intrigued when the fat, ungainly Bert turned out to be a creditable ballet dancer.

When he was demobilized, Russell went to London, where Bert secured squalid lodgings for him. Though he had no experience in art, he managed to convince the owner of an art gallery to give him a job as salesperson. Here, in 1948, he met the two Scottish painters, Robert McBryde and Robert Colquhoun. He was later to do a film about them for the BBC.

Russell joined the same ballet club to which Bert belonged, but realizing that there was no future with this group of amateurs, he applied for a scholarship to the International Ballet's school. Since male dancers were scarce, he was successful. He was quite old for a beginner, not in good shape, and rather terrible, but he executed one incredible jump which won over the Russian dancing master. However, he never improved and was prone to injuries, so the company eventually asked him to leave.

He joined a touring company of <u>Annie Get Your Gun</u> whose entire male chorus was high camp. He later secured a job at the British Dance Theatre, which specialized in psychological ballets; then he joined the London Theatre Ballet, which performed at seaside resorts. He was half of the male <u>corps de ballet</u>. In a production of <u>Coppélia</u> he was given the part of Dr. Coppelius because it entailed little dancing; his interpretation of the doctor as a <u>Caligari</u>-esque madman was unmemorable.

He joined the Norwegian Ballet, which was desperate for dancers, and again appeared in <u>Coppélia</u>, this time as a doll. Returning to England, he knew he would never succeed as a dancer, so he tried acting. He was not very good at that, either; he then decided to try photography, and enrolled in classes at the Walthamstow Art School. At last he was really good at something, although his visual imagination was rather bizarre for fashion photography--his chosen field. After failing to find jobs in either fashion or advertising, Russell worked free-lance.

In 1956 Russell made a silent film called <u>Peepshow</u>, and took it to the British Film Institute in the hope of receiving a grant sufficient to finish it properly. He did not receive the grant, but as a result of this effort became acquainted with a man who interested him in Catholicism. He was entranced by the idea of the symbolic eating of Christ's body. He sought religious instruction at a nearby convent and was converted. For a few years he was an avid Catholic; then he gradually began to reject some of the Church's beliefs. Nevertheless, the experience left him with a sense of purpose, strength and confidence which he would not otherwise have had.

At Walthamstow Russell had met Shirley Kingdon, a fashion design student; they married in February 1957. On their honeymoon they went to the Yorkshire moors and did a photo essay on the Brontës, with Shirley, in Victorian costumes, playing all three sisters.

Also in 1957, while he was still an enthusiastic Catholic, Russell set about making a Catholic film, and quickly discovered that the Catholic Film Institute--the pretentious title given to a one-man office in a basement--would be little help to him financially. But its director, Tony Evans, volunteered to help him shoot the film. Evans, Russell, and Shirley shot <u>Amelia and the Angel</u> for £300 plus a £150 loan from the British Film Institute.

The Russells went to Lourdes, and Ken decided to do a film about it. Through a series of lucky breaks, the film was made fairly cheaply, but Russell was unable to sell it. He took it and <u>Amelia</u> to the BBC's Assistant Head of Films, Norman Swallow, who was enthusiastic and found him a job doing documentaries on the <u>Monitor</u> series

3

under the aegis of Huw Wheldon. Russell was very happy making filmlets on a wide variety of topics in the arts. The filmlets gradually became longer, more flamboyant, more controversial, more sophisticated. Russell met many of the technical and acting talents with whom he would continue to work in feature films.

Critical Survey of Oeuvre

There is no doubt that Ken Russell is one of the most consistently controversial filmmakers of the seventies. Some critics consider his work infuriating, abrasive, excessive, insufferable, and even nauseating. Others find it hilarious, endearing, moving, and brilliant. One can hear all these epithets applied to the same film, sometimes to the same scene. Objectivity is impossible; his advocates love every excessive scene, while his detractors tend to consider everything he does as ineffable trash.

Many of Russell's severest critics are "music lovers" who object to the quixotic and highly personal interpretations Russell attaches to the lives and works of his composer subjects. Filming life stories is a tricky business at best--someone is always likely to be offended--but when Russell's sensationalist touch compels him to dwell on the most sordid aspects of his subjects' lives, the results are explosive. There are repercussions from morally indignant critics, from The Society for Whichever-Composer-It-Is-This-Time, and from ordinary people who prefer Hollywood's absurd, romantic distortions to Russell's biographies--often equally absurd and distorted, but infinitely less soothing.

In any case, Russell's focus is not so much on the facts of an artist's life as on the way life influences art and art, life. His references to more concrete aspects of his subjects' lives tend to be oblique, while the opinions expressed in his films are personal and highly unorthodox. For purposes of clarity and balance, it is helpful to read the artist's biography before seeing a Russell biopic.

Russell's methods are as outrageous as his results. His treatment of actors is sometimes rough and always demanding. Nevertheless, he has acquired a solid repertory company which has included Oliver Reed, Glenda Jackson, the late Max Adrian, Roger Daltrey, and innumerable character actors, including Vladek Sheybal, Christopher Gable, Robert Powell, Izabella Telezynska and Judith Paris. Most of these started working with Russell during his ten-year television career.

Russell began working in television in 1959. On the strength of a couple of amateur films, he was hired to film short features on artistic people for the Monitor program, supervised by Huw Wheldon for the British Broadcasting Corporation. Some of his subjects in those early years were Lotte Lenya, art nouveau architect Antonio Gaudi, Spike Milligan of Goon Show fame, choreographer John Cranko, playwright Shelagh Delaney, and composer Serge Prokofiev. Most of these films were about ten minutes long, but they gradually increased in length; Elgar (1962) is fifty minutes long, and some of the later ones are feature-length.

Russell overcame a rather formidable obstacle when he was allowed to use actors in his documentaries. (The BBC apparently had feared that actors portraying real historical figures, but speaking fabricated dialog in a documentary format, would lend a sort of spurious authenticity to his flights of biographical fancy—much as the newscast form of Welles' War of the Worlds gave it believability.) He eased gently into the use of actors: in the Prokofiev film, he used an actor's hands; in Elgar, the actors were allowed to be seen from a distance but not to speak; in The Debussy Film the actors played both themselves and Debussy's circle. Finally the documentaries began to look like feature films, with screenplays and a lot of directorial license.

Dante's Inferno (1967), about the Pre-Raphaelite poet-painter Dante Gabriel Rossetti, is an impressive example of the Russell approach to documentary and to biography. Having a fondness for authenticity, Russell chose actors (in some cases non-professionals) who resembled the Pre-Raphaelites he was discussing; the effect is striking and rather eerie. Oliver Reed, while not Rossetti's double, captures the essence of Russell's interpretation while providing the right kind of voice for poetry recitation. The supporting players, chosen for their resemblance to Rossetti's subjects, look like his canvases come to life. As elsewhere, Russell implies rather than states useful information; Rossetti's housekeeper's cryptic remark in one scene that "the armadilly's arrived" is Russell's way of saying that Rossetti kept a menagerie. He tends to use the facts of his subjects' lives only when they provide a springboard for his incredible visual imagination. In this case, the menagerie gives him an excuse to use iguanas and other incongruous animals to represent the unhealthier aspects of the Pre-Raphaelites.

The Russell documentary-biography has one other feature which distinguishes it from the rest of the genre: the artist's work is introduced and displayed almost casually in the context of the screenplay rather than being reverently paraded for the audience's inspection. In Dante's Inferno, drawings and paintings are spread over the studio walls to be noticed in passing; Rossetti's poetry is used to illuminate scenes from his life. In the composer films, music is used in a similar manner, to illustrate or comment on the composer's emotional life.

6

Russell did several daring films during the last half of his BBC career. Song of Summer (1968), about the blind, paralyzed Frederick Delius, won almost unanimous acclaim. It is uncharacteristically subdued and lyrical, yet it explores with rather harrowing thoroughness Russell's recurring themes of the creative artist as destructive egoist and the irreconcilable differences between the artist's life and his art. Like so many of the people Russell has studied, Delius, the composer of sublime music, was actually impossible to live with due to the syphilis he had caught in an extramarital affair. His demands made a wreck of his young amanuensis, Eric Fenby. Russell's film was lauded for the subtlety with which he portrayed the relationship between these two men.

The final BBC film, The Dance of the Seven Veils (1970), was not well received. Conceived as a "comic strip" on the life of Richard Strauss, it contains a good deal of the Russell overstatement, as well as some outright pornography. Critical consensus was that Russell had gone over the top in this scathing condemnation of that which he considered shallow and Fascist in Strauss's life and music. This was Russell's last TV work. During his stay at the BBC he made TV documentary virtually an art form while developing the style he was to use to such effect in his feature films.

During the BBC period Russell also made some commercials (some of them, for beans, soap, and candy, later come in for savage parody in Tommy) and a couple of feature films. The first, French Dressing (1963), is a minor comedic effort which drew little critical attention beyond a few remarks about the promise Russell showed. His first major feature was Billion Dollar Brain (1968), sequel to the successful Harry Palmer spy films, Funeral in Berlin and The Ipcress File. It suffers in comparison with its predecessors, partially because it is rather fanciful and James Bondian, while the first two are basically (and refreshingly) realistic. The one sequence that drew critical notice is a battle on the ice which is an obvious, and by most accounts well-done, homage to a similar scene in Eisenstein's Alexander Nevsky.

Russell's film of D. H. Lawrence's Women in Love confirmed early predictions that he would be an important filmmaker. Most critics liked the movie; many of these felt that Russell's film had come as close to the spirit of the complex novel as any film could. Somehow Russell had found visual and aural equivalents to Lawrence's lush, intense, erotic, and sometimes downright purple prose. While preserving much of the novel's structure, he managed to find ways to deal with Lawrence's more difficult and controversial ideas. Some of the "big" scenes in the book could easily become ludicrous on screen: Gerald Crich subjugating his terrified horse at a railroad crossing; Gudrun Brangwen dancing provocatively for a herd of cattle; Rupert Birkin plunging naked through a forest; Crich snowshoeing to his death in the Alps. Russell plays these straight, preserving their dramatic impact. Likewise, some of Lawrence's ideas about sexuality,

7

particularly his quest for a sort of "higher friendship" between males, require a gentle touch to avoid campiness. The ultimate expression of physical closeness between men, the firelit wrestling match, is the best example of Russell's sensitivity to the Lawrence material. At the time of the film's release, this sequence was rather a cause célèbre--mostly among people who hadn't seen it--because of its pioneering use of frontal male nudity; in actuality the scene is beautifully and movingly done, erotic without being lewd.

Russell came under fire for a few omissions and lapses. He had left out Lawrence's long account of Birkin's and Crich's sojourn among some Bohemian London friends as well as some less significant episodes which, while restating Lawrence's philosophy, do little to advance the plot. The character of Hermione Roddice, treated in the book with a certain amount of compassion, becomes in the film a figure of fun. There are various major and minor "betrayals" of Lawrence. However, Russell and his screenwriter, Larry Kramer, added several rather inspired visual and verbal touches, such as the shock cut from Birkin's and Ursula Brangwen's post-coital embrace to that of the drowned lovers in Crich's lake, and the interpolation of an off-color Lawrentian dissertation on the womanliness of figs into a genteel garden party scene.

The cast served Russell well. Alan Bates, besides resembling Lawrence, is excellent as the complex, idealistic-cynical, semi-autobiographical Birkin character. Glenda Jackson is Gudrun to the life, with her coolness, intelligence, eroticism, and destructive kink. Some critics were not so well-pleased with Oliver Reed and Jennie Linden; this was due more to their appearance than their ability. Reed, while nothing like the near-Aryan man-god of the novel, portrays the stodgy, repressed, tormented, doomed Crich with subtlety; and Linden overcomes a disconcerting perkiness to do justice to the difficult role of Ursula, who cannot understand her husband's need for a relationship with Crich in addition to their marriage.

1971 saw three films released. The first, The Music Lovers, revealed the wilder side of Russell and made it obvious that Women in Love would be the last film for quite a while to win praise for good taste. Viewers in Britain, who had seen some of the BBC films, were probably more prepared than American audiences for Russell's flamboyant version of, or, more nearly, attack on the life and art of Peter Tchaikovsky. The raw material for the film was already sensational, as Russell pointed out to the backers--the story of a homosexual composer, married to a nymphomaniac, with elements of fetishism, death by boiling, incest, and insanity.

Russell does more than justice to the plot, exploiting to the utmost the extraordinary aspects of Tchaikovsky's life. To do this, a good deal of distortion was necessary. Russell heightens the effect of the film by showing Tchaikovsky's wife Nina writhing in an abbatoir-like madhouse in mid-film; in actuality, she was not put there until after Tchaikovsky's death. Russell also rearranges Peter's relationship with his patroness, Madame Nadezhda von Meck. She is shown creeping into his room while he sleeps and lying down beside him, although there is no evidence that they ever saw one another. Russell also pins the severance of Mme. von Meck's patronage on the revelation of Tchaikovsky's sexual preferences by his lover, Count Anton Chiluvsky--once more, without textual evidence. A final liberty portrays Tchaikovsky committing suicide by drinking cholera-infected water while thinking of his mother, who had died horribly in a boiling bath--the cure in extremis for cholera. The manner of his death is accurate enough; the motive is conjecture. Still, even these blatant liberties can be excused in part by the fact that Russell never claims historical accuracy. The viewer of a Russell film can expect, at worst (barring physical illness), to be sufficiently piqued to want to examine other versions, or at best, to become turned-on to the subject's work. (A popularized biography is better than none; perhaps it is better to think of Tchaikovsky as looking like Richard Chamberlain than not to think of him at all.)

Mixed with the hyperbole is a good deal of Russell's brand of historic narrative, and several wild fantasy sequences using Tchaikovsky's music. Russell set out to make an anti-romantic movie, a sort of antithesis to the Night and Day kind of biopic which presents the artist's "Greatest Hits" in a way that suggests they sprang into his mind fully grown and orchestrated. To do this Russell gives the standard Hollywood clichés some new finales: a soft-focus, slow-motion romantic idyll has as characters Tchaikovsky and his sister; Peter finishes his last symphony, which is about his life, and announces he'll call it the Tragic--his brother Modeste sneers, correctly, that Pathetic would be closer to the truth. Russell also uses Tchaikovsky's "Greatest Hit"--the stirring but far from subtle 1812 Overture; like most composers' best known works, it is considered musically inferior to almost everything else he ever wrote. In one of the film's most discussed sequences, Tchaikovsky is seen perched on a mosque, conducting his most popular work with savage glee; with each cannon shot he fantasizes that he blows the head off one of the people in his life. (This is an echo of a parallel scene in the Rossetti film.) Meanwhile, brother Modeste rakes in piles of royalty money from the 1812.

The Music Lovers alienated many critics who had been favorably impressed by Women in Love; the actors also suffered at their hands. Richard Chamberlain, who had just begun to shake off his "Dr. Kildare" stigma by means of a very creditable TV Hamlet, received mixed notices for his portrayal of Tchaikovsky; aside from a few extreme love/hate opinions, he was generably considered to have done as well as could be expected in a bad film. Glenda Jackson as Nina fared little better.

A positive aspect of The Music Lovers was that it continued the tradition Russell had begun with Women in Love--that of making a very low-budget film look very rich. This would be a Russell trademark throughout his career; for this he owed, and owes, a great deal to his staff. He had craftily secured the services of one of the best costumiers around by marrying her; Shirley Russell's costumes are sometimes the highlight of his films. He is equally blessed by the low turnover in his design and cinematography crews.

Another Russell characteristic which began to be a motif in his films is the influence of music and dance on even non-musical films. This is evident to a certain extent in Women in Love, more so in The Music Lovers. Russell always has a choreographer; he always includes carefully plotted mimetic sequences.

Critic Gene Siskel wrote recently that Russell's big problem is that "an outlandish scene grabs the public's attention, and the film is lost for those who can't see past their outrage."[1] This was certainly true of The Devils, which drew some of the most vitriolic comment ever written. Oddly, in a year which produced A Clockwork Orange and Straw Dogs, The Devils was roundly condemned by all but a few iconoclasts for its ugliness, pornography, and violence. Based on John Whiting's play and Aldous Huxley's nonfiction work, The Devils of Loudun, it is the story of an outbreak of religio-erotic hysteria in a seventeenth-century convent, which culminated in the burning of a blameless priest for witchcraft. The Huxley book is a relentless illustration of how an insignificant incident was turned into a tragic cause célèbre due to the machinations of the Church under Cardinal Richelieu; Russell kept fairly close to Huxley's narrative. Several graphic and rather blasphemous sequences have given the film the reputation of being anti-Church--justly, since in this case the Church was the villain. The film is generally against any organization--church, state, or otherwise-- powerful enough to corrupt and distort without censure.

Seldom has Russell had to alter his source so little for shock effect. It is all there in the heavily-documented book: big issues --corruption, political games-playing, the terrible ignorance of the time, the persecution of a man who made the wrong enemies--but also details--the effeminacy of the King, the methods of torture, the incredible "possession" of the Ursuline nuns, the rites of exorcism. Russell has been called to account for showing the nuns being given enemas of holy water with a device that looks like the bastard off- spring of a grease gun and a fire extinguisher. In fact, this clyster, as it was called, was widely used to treat a plethora of ills. Of course, it is one thing to read Huxley's account of clyster-

---

1. "The Big Scene Grabber Hits Again in the Movie Tommy," Chicago Tribune (25 March 1975), Section 3, p. 2.

ing and quite another to see a demonstration. Most of the abuse
heaped on Russell for this film stems from his willingness to show
everything, a circumstance shared by the film of The Exorcist.
("They couldn't possibly have filmed the next part of the book," we
murmur, seconds before gallons of Campbell's best split pea festoon
a far wall.) Russell's admitted purpose in filming The Devils was
to arouse people who had become desensitized to pain and suffering,
to make it impossible for them to remain passive; this has always
been one of his purposes, although his methods here are more brutal
than most. Russell has claimed he used restraint by not showing
the worst of the tortures endured by the doomed priest Grandier.
This claim rings rather hollow considering that he omitted little
else. Nonetheless, underneath all the grotesquerie, there is a
disturbing, moving, and visually beautiful film.

For a color film, especially a period one, The Devils is
remarkably austere. Russell chose to stylize the city of Loudun;
although there is enough muck and decay to depict the meanness of
living conditions, many of the scenes are played in rooms or outside buildings made of gleaming white bricks. Costumes are sub-
dued--black, white, and dashes of color. The effect is surreal--
we are reminded of de Chirico's empty cityscapes. We find evidence
of Russell's fondness for fantasy sequences in the strange, blasphemous erotic scenes filmed in grainy black and white. These, which
again resemble parts of Dante's Inferno, owe much to Ingmar Bergman
for their stylization, eerie imagery, and psychological evocative-
ness.

Critics were again unsure of how to discuss the acting jobs done
by Oliver Reed and Vanessa Redgrave. Her role, the instigator of
the trouble, Mother Jeanne of the Angels, was turned down by Glenda
Jackson who thought, rightly, that it would be another of the crazy
lady parts she had recently been offered. We can only guess at what
she would have done with the character; Redgrave gives Mother Jeanne
a sort of creepy birdlike feyness. It is effective in its way, but
more than a little embarrassing at times to watch, and hard to
assess. Her performance was deemed ridiculous, sublime and all
nuances between. Reed's portrayal of Grandier is less idiosyn-
cratic and more effective, making him a man of dignity and magnetism.
It was recognized as one of the best of his career--small consolation
for being shaved, bruised, and half-cooked during the filming. Both
actors were generally praised even by those critics who hated the
film.

After the rigors of shooting The Devils, Russell and his crew
undertook The Boy Friend as a sort of vacation. (Later Russell said
that perhaps the film would have been better if he had taken a
vacation from it entirely.) It is a marked departure from his
usual style and does not have the force or daring that we have come
to expect from him. Still, it is quite good. Russell has expanded
the plot of the Sandy Wilson boy-meets-girl musical comedy pastiche

by making it a play-within-a-film, adding a frame story about the actors performing the play at a run-down repertory playhouse with a big film producer in the audience. This allows Russell some good shots at not only theatrical clichés, but film ones as well-- including some unmistakable references to film musicals. Russell shot much of the film at a provincial theatre; the scenes onstage, during which the hollow clump of the actors' footsteps on the floorboards all but drown out their dialogue, have a hilarious authenticity.

Russell has always had a penchant for humor; by the nature of the films he had made before The Boy Friend, he had been able to display the black side of it (The Devils in particular is full of grim jokes). The Boy Friend, while retaining some nearly savage wit, also allows for some conventional humor. For some commentators this was a difficult blend: The film, neither straight nor satiric, drew fire from those who like their musicals to be either one or the other. Russell also indulges his fondness for film in-jokes: his expanded plot permits his use of the old Ruby Keeler device of the mousey assistant stage manager substituting for the injured star and "wowing 'em." He even manages to work in a scene in which the leading man removes the assistant stage manager's glasses and exclaims, "Why, you're beautiful!" And of course there's a joke on his own films in the person of Glenda Jackson, in a cameo appearance as the ailing star.

The most striking reference to other films involves the other addition to the plot, the scouting film director. As he watches the rather dispirited performance (in which the more ambitious members of the troupe try to upstage one another for his benefit), he fantasizes about the two young stars in a series of charming and sometimes dazzling film production numbers in the tradition of Busby Berkeley's MGM musicals. These are the most memorable scenes in The Boy Friend; although they lack the distinct Berkeley touch, they capture the general feel of the MGM set pieces. One features shiny black floors, tubular chrome, Art Deco motifs, silver lamé, and innumerable chorines in geometrical formations. Another uses oversized furniture, and yet another takes place in a sort of Alice-in-Wonderland, Babes-in-Toyland set. In a final in-joke, the director decides against filming The Boy Friend in favor of Singin' in the Rain.

Most of the actors in The Boy Friend are old Russell hands. Max Adrian plays the play's director, Max Mandeville; Vladek Sheybal is movie director De Thrill; and Murray Melvin and Antonia Ellis are members of the chorus. Russell took a chance on the two young leads. Christopher Gable, although he had appeared in several of Russell's films, was (and still is) nearly unknown at the box office. However, as a former Royal Ballet dancer, he executes the dance numbers with grace and style. He is also young and winsome. The biggest unknown element was the use of fashion model Leslie (Twiggy) Hornby, as the heroine, Polly Browne. Critics and public alike who had seen her

12

doll-like face and slight figure were skeptical about her acting
potential. The Boy Friend is a pleasant surprise in this respect.
While not a major personality, Twiggy is very sweet as the love-
struck assistant stage manager, warbling rather than singing her way
through "You Are My Lucky Star" and several other songs. In addition,
her dancing, while not outstanding, is surprisingly competent.

Once again, the décor of the film is nearly perfect. The theatre, costumes and general air of the seedy troupe are limp and worn,
providing even greater contrast with the sumptuousness of the fantasy sequences.

Savage Messiah (1972) is a throwback to Russell's more subdued
TV biographies. Its gentleness won back a few of the critics alienated by The Music Lovers and The Devils; characteristically, many
Russell aficionados found it less than fascinating. Russell himself
describes it as a story about two people in a room, talking. For
once Russell eschews his shock tactics and comes up with a quiet,
relatively straightforward account of the life of Henri Gaudier,
turn-of-the-century avant-garde sculptor, killed at twenty-three
in World War I, and his relationship with would-be writer Sophie
Brzeska, twenty years his senior. Russell tells their story--how
they met; formed an odd platonic relationship; lived together, pov-
erty-ridden in London, as brother and sister under their combined
surnames; hurt each other and parted; came together again--all with
a gentleness which surprised most who saw the film. The one scene
which was singled out for praise is one in which Gaudier asks an
art dealer to come to see his new sculpture the next day. He has
no sculpture, but he, Sophie, and a friend steal a gravestone and
he carves away all night long, expounding on life, art, and their
relationship every minute of the time. This relationship, of course,
is a standard Russell theme, but seldom has he put it across with
such lucidity and tolerance.

Once again, Russell produced a visually beautiful film, this
time without the spellbinding tricks that are his trademark. And
once again his principals are virtual unknowns. His Gaudier is
newcomer Scott Antony, chosen after character actor John McEnery
proved to photograph too old. Sophie is played by Dorothy Tutin
who, although one of England's most distinguished stage actresses,
is nearly unknown to U.S. audiences (her last major film had been
The Importance of Being Earnest in 1952). Both performances were
praised; Tutin's in particular is complex, emotional and haunting.
It impressed even hardened Russell detractors.

Mahler (1974) is, in comparison, a return to the old, outrageous mold, extreme, idiosyncratic--and beautiful. Virtually
unseen in the States, except in art houses and on college campuses,
the film was mercilessly panned by the majority of British and
Continental critics. While not as frantic as The Devils and The
Music Lovers, it has its share of weird scenes--the depiction of

Mahler's conversion from Judaism as a cross between the Siegfried legend and Laurel and Hardy; a living cremation; a savage swipe at Cosima Wagner (foreshadowing Lisztomania).

However, parts of the film are restrained, simple, emotionally rich. Particularly poignant is Russell's expression of Alma's hurt at Gustav's contempt for her composition: she is seen putting the manuscripts of her songs in a small coffin and sadly burying them. Similarly, the reconciliation at the end, accompanied by a fulsome Mahler melody, may be the kind of "schmaltz" The Music Lovers ridicules, but it is enjoyable nonetheless.

As usual, the performances of the nearly unknown lead actors are very good. Robert Powell, who has recently distinguished himself as Christ in Zeffirelli's Jesus of Nazareth, makes a sensitive, vulnerable, irascible, difficult Mahler (besides closely resembling him). Georgina Hale, a Russell regular, transcends a rather annoying nasal tone to portray Alma with perception and sensitivity.

Tommy (1975) was a total departure for Russell. He had never indicated that he acknowledged the existence of rock music; he had once listened to the Who's rock opera and thought it rubbish. However, he did film it and has been rewarded by its monetary, popular, and critical success. Most critics agreed that Russell had found his perfect subject, and that Tommy's pop-culture vulgarity lent itself admirably to his methods. The compliment was left-handed but accurate.

The plot of the Peter Townshend opera is excessively simple, but its message is muddled. Townshend says its theme is connected with the teachings of the mystic, Meher Baba, although this does not prevent each viewer from imposing his own meanings on it. Actually, it doesn't hold up well under serious scrutiny (the references to LSD, for instance, seem strangely dated); it is much more satisfying when viewed superficially as a multimedia assault on the senses.

The entire film is removed from reality. The sets and costumes are gorgeously stylized; the plot advances in a series of set-pieces whose visual styles vary. The "Pinball Wizard" sequence is bright and glittery; the "I'm a Sensation" segment is quiet and naturalistic; the sequences with Cousin Kevin and Uncle Ernie have a nightmarelike quality. Russell's active (some would say febrile) imagination accounts for a two-hour procession of these one-song set pieces, each contributing unforgettable images. Among the best are Nora's orgasmic freak-out amid disgusting goo; the Pinball Wizard with his outlandish costume (one of countless brilliant Shirley Russell creations); Tommy's exhilarating flight on a hang-glider; the recurring image of Tommy's father holding a globe of light.

The acting is also stylized. Since much of it is done by non-
acting rock stars, this is fortunate. Each performer "does his own
thing" and it works well for Russell's purposes. Particularly good
are Tina Turner's crazy, incredibly bestial Acid Queen, Eric Clapton's
stoned-out Monroe priest, Paul Nicholas' schizoid Cousin Kevin, and
Keith Moon's hilarious rubber-gloved, garter-belted Uncle Ernie.

The three pivotal roles of Tommy, Frank and Nora require a
certain amount of acting skill. Russell took a bit of a risk casting film newcomer Roger Daltrey as Tommy, but he needed a strong
rock singer with some charisma whose vocal style matched Townshend's
music. Daltrey was the obvious choice. Most of his performance
consists of "selling" songs, and he does that very well. He is also
good in physically difficult scenes, such as his flight from the
burning holiday camp and his run through the junkyard. He jumps
through flames, lurches into car doors, falls down, and generally
takes punishment with equanimity.

In the role of Frank, Oliver Reed establishes himself as one
of the least self-conscious actors and one of the most blatant non-
singers in films. He makes Frank wonderfully slimy, supremely
greedy, yet not utterly unlikeable. Ann-Margret has the most difficult task, having not only to age twenty-five years but also to run
the gamut of emotions and of spiritual states. (One unknown com-
mentator remarked, intriguingly and accurately, that one can trace
Nora's moral decline by watching her eye-shadow.) Hers is a bravura
job of acting, and a courageous one as well; most of the time she is
photographed unflatteringly and looks like a has-been hooker. Her
sheer stamina is also commendable, considering that she endured a
week of wallowing in cold beans and chocolate for the sake of a few
highly charged minutes on screen. Also impressive, in a small part,
is Robert Powell as Tommy's ethereal-looking father.

The film uses an experimental sound system, Quintaphonic, in
which instrumental tracks are played through four speakers at the
sides of the movie theatre, while vocals come from a speaker at
the front. The system has its drawbacks. Generally it works well
in large theatres and ones which can afford to install the best
equipment--mainly large showcases in major cities. The system
and the film fare worse in smaller theatres, which rent portable
equipment. Often these theatres have neither the resources nor the
staff to insure that the system is running properly or that the
volume is not injurious. When the system is working well, the
quality of the soundtrack is astounding.

Lisztomania (1975) is another of the totally outrageous type of
Russell film. As usual, its look is sumptuous and the costumes
inspired--a dressing gown with piano-key collar and a Pope's vest-
ment decorated with movie-star photos are among them. However, the
film's structure is less tight and its flights of fancy less evoca-
tive than those of his other films.

Russell here finishes off the assault on Richard Wagner and his wife Cosima (Liszt's daughter) begun in Mahler. Wagner is portrayed as a vampire, feeding off Liszt's talent for the sake of his own. (More than one critic has speculated that Russell may, in this respect, identify with Wagner, since he himself has made his reputation from others' lives.) Later he is a satanist-mad-scientist-Nazi, and is reborn as a Frankenstein monster-Hitler. Cosima is shown sticking pins into a voodoo doll of her father. Their Aryan superman is portrayed as a moronic, beer-swilling, anti-social Golem who spouts anti-Semitism by rote and urinates on the floor.

Once again the principal is Daltrey, who is less effective than he is in Tommy. The songs he sings are undistinguished rearrangements of Liszt by Rick Wakeman; while competent as an actor, he has neither the means nor the opportunity to give Liszt any dramatic depth. The film has little to do with Liszt's actual life and art, and it is nearly incomprehensible—but it is a great deal of fun to watch.

Valentino (1977) marks the meeting of two of show business' greatest egos—Russell's and Rudolf Nureyev's. The resulting film displays a good deal of both. As usual, the film is opulent, beautifully photographed, dramatically powerful—but ambiguous. Russell's intent seems to have been to portray Valentino as a man who is manipulated by people, primarily women. This is evidenced by some symbolic shots in which Nazimova's shadow obliterates his projected image, and one in which Rambova assures Rudy that a film will be the product "of one person—us." The film is Russell's usual mixture of fact, fiction, conjecture and overstatement, but he seems not to have reckoned with his star's force of character.

In Nureyev, Russell has the perfect actor to play Valentino. The dancer has the same kind of smouldering good looks, the catlike grace, the arrogance, the sex appeal, that Valentino is said to have possessed. His Valentino is less a pawn than a man whose love and naiveté lead him to rash and sometimes damaging acts, and who possesses an innate dignity and panache. The character is more sympathetic than most Russell targets.

As usual, the film says little about its subject, but much about Russell; the main difference is that it also says things about Nureyev—seldom has Russell allowed an actor to dominate a film as he does here. Nureyev proves himself capable of fighting, dancing, making love, and generally playing his two-and-a-half dimensional character with style and variety.

Few others in the film get a chance to portray more than cardboard cutouts; Felicity Kendal and Seymour Cassell as Rudy's faithful friends come closest with restrained, sincere performances. Leslie Caron is properly superficial as the melodramatic Nazimova,

but Michelle Phillips fails to bring Natasha Rambova to emotional
life. At worst, the film is still another extravagant, inaccurate
Valentino biopic; at best it is visually beautiful and entertaining.

Russell has many prospects for future projects. Some of the
longer-standing ones are a George Gershwin biopic starring Neil
Diamond, another film with Daltrey, and one about Thomas à Becket
with Oliver Reed. Whether he chooses one of these or a totally
different subject for his next cinematic extravaganza, the result
will certainly be far from boring.

Film Synopses and Credits

1   FRENCH DRESSING (Great Britain, 1963)

    Jim, deck-chair concessionaire at the less-than-thriving spa of Gormleigh-on-Sea, has an idea to improve business. He has seen how events like film festivals, with visiting actresses like Bardot, have benefited continental resorts like St. Tropez. Along with his friend Henry and his girl Judy, he convinces the Mayor to hold a film festival with French star Françoise Fayol as guest. Fayol attracts quite a crowd and Jim is enamored with her. Judy becomes jealous.

    The climax of the festival is to be a showing of the latest Fayol skin flick. It is interrupted by a riot which has been instigated by the mayors of the neighboring resort towns whose business Gormleigh has stolen.

    Françoise, angered, returns to France and her ex-boyfriend, leaving Gormleigh without anyone to open its new Nudist Beach. Judy, wearing the blonde wig Françoise has left, substitutes for her. No one notices the switch in the pouring rain, and as the nude Judy enters the sea, Jim and Henry come along and pull her out. The three stroll away, unmindful of the threats of the irate Mayor of Gormleigh.

Credits:

Director:	Ken Russell
Producer:	Kenneth Harper (Kenwood Films)
Associate Producer:	Andrew Mitchell
Screenplay:	Peter Myers, Ronald Cass, Peter Brett, from an original story by Myers and Cass
Additional Dialogue:	Johnny Speight
Photography:	Ken Higgins
Sound:	Norman Coggs, Len Shilton
Music:	Composed and directed by Georges Delerue
Art Director:	Jack Stephens
Editor:	Jack Slade

Cast: James Booth (Jim), Roy Kinnear
                                           (Henry), Marisa Mell (Françoise
                                           Fayol), Alita Naughton (Judy),
                                           Bryan Pringle (The Mayor), Robert
                                           Robinson (Himself), Norman Pitt
                                           (Westbourne Mayor), Henry McCarthy
                                           (Bridgemouth Mayor), Sandor Eles
                                           (Vladek)
Distribution: Warner/Pathé
Running time: 86 minutes (7,730 feet)
Released: 20 May 1964 (London)

*2   BILLION DOLLAR BRAIN (Great Britain, 1967)

Harry Palmer is determined to stay retired from espionage.
He takes a freelance assignment to bring a canister of eggs
to Helsinki, where he is to deliver them to a Dr. Kaarna.
Anya, Kaarna's contact, takes him to the doctor, who turns
out to be a friend of Harry's, agent Leo Newbegin. Newbegin
belongs to a violently anti-Commie organization run by the
American millionaire, General Midwinter. When Harry discovers that the real Kaarna has been murdered, he is drugged
and kidnapped by members of his old group, MI5, who threaten
to implicate him in Kaarna's death if he doesn't do some
snooping for them about the eggs and Midwinter.

The eggs, Harry discovers, are impregnated with a lethal
virus which Midwinter hopes to use to incite rebellion within
Russia and in her satellite countries. He has a billion-dol-
lar computer which plans and orders all his maneuvers; it is
housed at Midwinter's center of operations in Latvia. Harry
goes there and finds out that Newbegin has been embezzling
from Midwinter. He also meets his old nemesis and friend,
the Russian agent Colonel Stok.

The computer orders Newbegin to kill Anya, whom it considers to be unreliable. Newbegin fails to dispose of her
and, to cover up, tries to erase the order from the computer's
tapes before he and Harry are taken to Texas to meet Midwinter.
Anya, who is a Russian agent, turns Leo over to Harry, fleeing
back to Russia and Stok with the eggs.

Midwinter, who is quite mad, won't accept the idea that
Latvia isn't ripe for insurrection and sends his army across
the frozen Baltic. The army is destroyed by bombs and swal-
lowed by the sea. Harry, the sole survivor, is rescued by
Anya and Stok, who, as a gesture of goodwill, hand the eggs
to him. He returns with them to MI5, hoping for a raise.

Credits:
Director: Ken Russell
Producer: Harry Saltzman (Lowndes Productions)
Executive Producer: Andre de Toth

Screenplay: John McGrath, based on the Len
                                Deighton novel
Photography: Billy Williams (Panavision; color
                                by Technicolor)
Cameraman: David Harcourt
Sound Mixer: John Mitchell
Music: Composed and directed by Richard
                                Rodney Bennett
Production Designer: Syd Cain
Art Director: Bert Davey
Editor: Alan Osbiston
Production Manager: Eva Monley
Assistant Directors: Jack Causey, Jim Brennan
Continuity: Angela Martelli
Makeup: Freddie Williamson, Benny Royston
Hairstyles: Joan Smallwood
Costumes: Shirley Russell
Wardrobe Supervisor: John Brady
Wardrobe Mistress: Maggie Lewin
Cast: Michael Caine (Harry Palmer), Karl
                                Malden (Leo Newbegin), Françoise
                                Dorleac (Anya), Oscar Homolka
                                (Colonel Stok), Ed Begley (General
                                Midwinter), Guy Doleman (Colonel
                                Ross), Vladek Sheybal (Dr. Eiwort),
                                Milo Sperber (Basil), Mark Elwes
                                (Birkinshaw), Stanley Caine (GPO
                                delivery boy)
Filmed on location in
Helsinki and Latvia.
Distribution: United Artists
Running time: 111 minutes (9,990 feet)
Released: November 1967 (London)

3   WOMEN IN LOVE (Great Britain, 1969)

   The time is just after World War I; the place, the mining
town of Beldover in the Midlands of England. The emancipated
Brangwen sisters live there in a middle-class dwelling with
their parents. Ursula is a schoolteacher, and Gudrun is an
artist who has spent some time in London. While discussing
their ambivalence toward love and marriage, they walk by the
church in time to see Laura Crich, daughter of Beldover's
wealthiest mineowner, arrive to be married to Tibby Lupton.
Watching the wedding party, Gudrun is fascinated by Laura's
brother Gerald, while Ursula is attracted by his friend Rupert
Birkin, who is the district school inspector.

Soon afterward, Birkin stops in at Ursula's classroom. As he points out the sexuality of the pussywillows the class is drawing, he is joined by Hermione Roddice, an affected and rather silly woman with whom he has a deteriorating relationship. Hermione invites Ursula and Gudrun to a house party, along with Rupert, Gerald, the newlyweds, and a few others. As they dine under the trees, Birkin shocks some and amuses others of the party when he peels a fig, discoursing on its erotic femaleness. In the evening, Hermione devises a sort of free-form Russian ballet in which Ursula and Gudrun must take part. The small audience, particularly Birkin, can't take it seriously; he instructs the pianist to change the tempo to ragtime. When he follows the infuriated Hermione into the next room, she brains him with a small blunt object. Bloody and a little dazed, he runs into the nearby woods and discards his clothes, enjoying his sensual communion with nature.

One day, walking, the Brangwen sisters come upon Gerald, on a highly-strung horse, approaching a railway crossing. The train comes and the horse tries to back off; Gerald uses whip and spurs to make the frantic animal hold firm. Gudrun is stimulated, Ursula appalled.

The Criches give their annual water-party, to which rich and poor alike are invited. Finding a peaceful, secluded spot, Ursula begins to sing while Gudrun, startlingly, performs a provocative dance for some longhorn cattle. Gerald runs to restrain her; she dances for him and nearly swoons in his grasp. Afterward, he declares his love for her. Toward evening, when several boating parties are on the small lake, Gerald discovers that Laura, who has been swimming, has gone under and that Tibby, trying to save her, has also disappeared. Gerald and the other men fruitlessly search for them. He arranges to have the sluice gates opened and the lake drained. Rupert and Ursula, oppressed by the air of tragedy, find a peaceful copse of trees and unexpectedly make love. When the lake is drained, Laura's body is found tightly clinging to Tibby's, her arms around his neck. Gerald says, "She killed him."

To relieve Gerald's tension following these events, Rupert, at their next meeting, challenges him to a bout of Japanese wrestling. In the parlor of Gerald's home, they strip, grapple at some length in the firelight, and finally collapse on the carpet. Both men have enjoyed the physical union. Rupert, who feels confined by the possibility of only man-woman love, wants a deep, eternal emotional union with a man as well. He hopes that the wrestling match will be a sort of affirmation of this sort of union with Gerald. Gerald, who feels that his capacity for love is limited, cannot understand this wish of Birkin's and therefore cannot commit to it. Rupert and Ursula continue their courtship. One day they have a vicious fight which ends in reconciliation and their decision to marry.

Gudrun, who has been tutoring Gerald's little sister Winifred in art, continues to see him. One night his father, who has been ill for some time, dies. Needing Gudrun, Gerald sneaks into the Brangwen house, makes love to her quietly, sleeps very heavily, and creeps out at dawn.

Ursula marries Birkin; they propose that Gudrun and Gerald accompany them to the Alps. At the hostel where they are staying, Gudrun meets Loerke, a homosexual artist, who draws her into conversation. He has some rather unwholesome-sounding ideas about the necessity for an artist to destroy what he loves; Gudrun is fascinated. Her relationship with Gerald, who dislikes Loerke, begins to decay. She sees it as a contest between them. Ursula finds herself at odds with the endless snow and cold, so Rupert takes her south to the Mediterranean.

Left with Gerald, Gudrun spends increasingly more time with Loerke, and considers going with him when he leaves the Tyrol for Dresden. Gerald is angry, hurt and jealous. The crisis comes one night when Gudrun insults and goads him into admitting he loves her--and then tells him she doesn't love him. A little later, as Gerald lies stonily in bed, she tries to arouse him sexually. He responds, taking her with bed-rocking violence.

The next day, when he comes upon Gudrun frolicking in the snow with Loerke, Gerald hits the smaller man and, seeing the look on Gudrun's face, starts to strangle her as well. He breaks off abruptly, says "I'm tired," and walks off toward the mountains. He travels for hours through the desolation until finally he stops, removes his gloves, and deliberately curls up to sleep.

When his body is found, Gudrun wires the Birkins, who return. Gudrun is calm, much more so than Rupert as he sits contemplating his friend's frozen face. He feels that if Gerald had accepted his offer of love, this would not have happened, or at least that his death would not have mattered, because his spirit would have lived on in Rupert. The Birkins and Gerald's body return to England; Gudrun joins Loerke in Dresden. One night, in their cottage in Beldover, Rupert reiterates his need for eternal union with a man as well as with Ursula. She has never understood this and says that she needs no one but him, therefore he should need no one but her. She tells him his yearning is perverse and impossible. He replies that he doesn't believe this.

Credits:

Director:	Ken Russell
Producers:	Larry Kramer and Martin Rosen (Brandywine Productions)
Associate Producer:	Roy Baird
Screenplay:	Larry Kramer, based on the novel by D. H. Lawrence

Photography:	Billy Williams (DeLuxe color)
Cameraman:	David Harcourt
Assistant Cameraman:	Stephen Claydon
Sound Editor:	Terry Rawlings
Sound Recorder:	Brian Simmons
Sound Re-recorder:	Maurice Askew
Music:	Composed and directed by Georges Delerue
Art Director:	Ken Jones
Set Decorators:	Luciana Arrighi, Harry Cordwell
Property Master:	George Ball
Construction:	Jack Carter
Editor:	Michael Bradsell
Choreographer:	Terry Gilbert
Production Manager:	Neville C. Thompson
Production Assistant:	Tom Erhardt
Assistant Director:	Jonathan Benson
Production Controller:	Harry Benn
Location Manager:	Lee Bolon
Continuity:	Angela Allen
Makeup:	Charles Parker
Hairstyles:	A. G. Scott
Costumes:	Shirley Russell
Wardrobe Supervisor:	Shura Cohn
Cast:	Alan Bates (Rupert Birkin), Oliver Reed (Gerald Crich), Glenda Jackson (Gudrun Brangwen), Jennie Linden (Ursula Brangwen), Eleanor Bron (Hermione Roddice), Michael Gough (Mr. Tom Brangwen), Norma Shebbeare (Mrs. Anna Brangwen), Alan Webb (Mr. Thomas Crich), Sharon Gurney (Laura Crich), Christopher Gable (Tibby Lupton), Nike Arrighi (Contessa), Vladek Sheybal (Loerke), Richard Heffer (Leitner), James Laurenson (Minister), Michael Graham Cox (Palmer), Leslie Anderson (Barber), Charles Workman (Gittens), Barrie Fletcher (First miner), Brian Osborne (Second miner), Christopher Ferguson (Basil Crich), Michael Garratt (Maestro), Richard Fitzgerald (Salsie)
Filmed on location in England at Derby, Sheffield, and Newcastle.	
Distribution:	United Artists
Running time:	130 minutes (11,672 feet)
Released:	November, 1969 (London)

24

4   THE MUSIC LOVERS (Great Britain, 1970)

In the winter of 1875, after a frolic with his lover, Count Anton Chiluvsky, Peter Tchaikovsky gives the first performance of his first piano concerto at the Moscow Conservatoire. His mentor, Rubinstein, is very critical, but the wealthy Nadezhda von Meck, a widow with a great passion for music, is in the audience and becomes interested in Tchaikovsky. She wishes to sponsor him, on the condition that they never meet. Peter is delighted with his good fortune and begins a voluminous correspondence with her, as he gives up teaching and devotes himself to composing.

His brother Modeste warns Peter that people are talking about him and Chiluvsky. Soon after writing the letter scene in Eugene Onegin, he is sent a similar letter by another woman from his Conservatoire audience, the impulsive, unstable Antonina Milyukova. Struck by the coincidence, Peter marries her in the hope of stilling the gossip. However, Antonina turns out to be a nymphomaniac. Her demands throw Peter into a breakdown and a suicide attempt even before their marriage is consummated.

He recuperates at Mme. von Meck's country estate, although the two still do not meet (aside from the widow stealing into his room to lie chastely beside him as he sleeps). For his birthday she throws an elaborate, fireworks-filled party. Chiluvsky turns up during this and is spurned by Tchaikovsky. He vindictively tells Mme. von Meck about Peter's sexual predilections; she terminates the relationship and withdraws her support.

Crushed, Peter nevertheless goes on to fame and fortune. But Antonina goes completely insane and is put into an asylum, and Peter's beloved sister Sasha turns against him. At the age of 53, haunted by visions of the people who have hurt him, he writes his sixth symphony. It embodies his life, and he wishes to call it the Tragic. Modeste snidely suggests that Pathetic is more to the point. Peter, whose memories of his mother's death are vivid, emulates her by purposely drinking a glass of cholera-ridden water. Undergoing the contemporary last-resort cure, he dies in a tub of boiling water.

Credits:

Director:	Ken Russell
Producer:	Ken Russell (Russfilms)
Executive Producer:	Roy Baird
Screenplay:	Melvin Bragg, based on the book Beloved Friend by Catherine Drinker Bowen and Barbara von Meck
Photography:	Douglas Slocombe (Panavision; color by Eastmancolor)
Cameraman:	Chick Waterson

Sound Editor:	Terry Rawlings
Sound Recorders:	Derek Ball, Maurice Askew
Music:	Peter Ilich Tchaikovsky: Performed by The London Symphony Orchestra
Musical Director:	Andre Previn
Musical Advisors:	Michael Moores, Elizabeth Corden
Soloists:	Piano--Raphael Orozco
	Mozart aria--April Cantelo
Production Designer:	Natasha Kroll
Art Director:	Michael Knight
Set Decorator:	Ian Whittaker
Editor:	Michael Bradsell
Choreographer:	Terry Gilbert
Production Manager:	Neville C. Thompson
Assistant Director:	Jonathan Benson
Unit Manager:	Graham Ford
Makeup:	George Frost
Hairstyles:	Ramon Gow, Patti Smith
Costumes:	Shirley Russell
Wardrobe Supervisor:	Elsa Fennell
Cast:	Richard Chamberlain (Peter Tchaikovsky), Glenda Jackson (Antonina Milyukova), Max Adrian (Nicholas Rubinstein), Christopher Gable (Count Anton Chiluvsky), Izabella Telezynska (Madame von Meck), Kenneth Colley (Modeste Tchaikovsky), Sabina Maydelle (Sasha Tchaikovsky), Maureen Pryor (Antonina's mother), Bruce Robinson (Alexei), Andrew Faulds (Davidov), Ben Aris (Young lieutenant), Joanne Brown (Olga Bredska), Imogen Claire (Lady in white), John and Dennis Myers (von Meck twins), Xavier Russell (Koyola), James Russell (Bobyek), Victoria Russell (Tatiana), Alexander Russell (Mme. von Meck's grandson), Alex Jawdokimov (Dmitri Shubelov), Clive Cazes (Doctor), Graham Armitage (Prince Balukin), Ernest Bale (Head waiter), Consuela Chapman (Tchaikovsky's mother), Alex Brewer (Young Tchaikovsky).
	Principal dancers for <u>Swan Lake</u> sequence: Georgina Parkinson (Odile), Alan Dubreuil (Prince Siegfried), Peter White (von Rothbart), Maggy Maxwell (Queen)

Filmed on location in England; interiors filmed at Bray Studios, Windsor.

Distribution: United Artists
Running time: 123 minutes (11,108 feet)
Released: 13 January 1971 (Los Angeles)

5   THE DEVILS (Great Britain, 1970)

In the France of the 1630's, the real power behind the effeminate Louis XIII is Cardinal Richelieu. In order to discourage divisive self-sufficiency among the walled towns of France, and thereby to keep the troublesome Huguenots in their place, he orders all city walls torn down. He sends an emissary, the Baron de Laubardemont, to defortify the plague-ridden town of Loudun. The parish priest, a secular Jesuit named Urbain Grandier, believes that the town should keep its walls and its self-sufficiency. With the authority given him by the now-deceased mayor of Loudun, Grandier delays the razing of the walls and petitions the King, who allows the walls to remain standing.

Grandier is a humane, enlightened man. As he comforts dying plague victims he is appalled at the ignorance and cruelty of the last-resort measures taken by the doctors. He is also a spiritually troubled man, not possessing the religious faith he preaches to others. His self-contempt because of this has become a death wish: where other men use power, wealth, and women to their advantage, he uses them as weapons against himself. This recklessness, combined with an argumentative nature, has made him several enemies in France, one of them Richelieu.

Grandier is young, handsome and sophisticated, and has seduced several female parishioners--in a quest, he mockingly tells another priest, to "come to God through the love of a woman." One of the girls, Phillipe Trinçant, becomes pregnant. When Grandier washes his hands of her, her father swears vengeance and allies himself with de Laubardemont. Grandier falls in love with another parishioner, young, devout Madeleine de Brou, and secretly marries her, playing the part of both bridegroom and priest. Despite the illicit nature of the ceremony, his bride is sure that they need fear no punishment from God. Grandier's most potent enemies, however, are mere men, as he soon learns.

Jeanne of the Angels, the hunchbacked Mother Superior of the town's Ursuline convent, has never met Grandier, but she sees him pass in a procession one day and develops a strong desire for him. She asks him to become the Ursulines' spiritual advisor after their old one dies, but Grandier refuses. Resentful because of this and jealous of Madeleine due to the rumors she has heard, she accuses him of being a warlock and of having plagued her with devils. An exorcist, the fanatical Father Barré, is called in. Jeanne puts on a strenuous, erotic

27

display of demonic possession--singularly unconvincing to the townspeople who support Grandier, but spectacular none-theless.

The extraordinary methods of exorcism, which include a holy-water enema, attract much attention; other nuns are ex-cited into frequent flamboyant displays of eroto-religious hysteria, which are further stimulated by de Laubardemont's threats of death if they cease. In the midst of a violent ex-hibition, the degenerate King, in the guise of the Duc de Condé, appears to give Barré a reliquary which he claims con-tains part of Christ's body. Upon hearing this, the "devils" quickly subside. When the King reveals that the reliquary is really empty, Grandier's persecution is shown to be an utter farce--one, however, which it amuses the jaded King not to interrupt.

Richelieu, who wishes Grandier's destruction, is anxious that he be proved guilty. Grandier, knowing the charges to be absurd, begins to realize his danger only when de Laubarde-mont has him tortured in the hope of forcing a confession. The priest knows that he has done this to himself through pride and wilfulness and self-contempt; he also knows, too late, that in Madeleine he now has a reason to live. He sees his doom approaching, and is able to accept it, gaining strength from self-knowledge.

Grandier defends himself admirably and eloquently, but a hand-picked court finds him guilty of the charges and sentences him to be burned. The Cardinal's agents know that they will look ridiculous without his confession, and accordingly sub-ject him to an "interrogation" during which the bones of his legs are systematically shattered. Somewhat to his own sur-prise, he finds himself unable to falsify a confession, even to spare himself this agony. Shaven and clothed in rags, he is made to crawl through the streets to his pyre. Jeanne, belatedly realizing what she has done, tries to recant but is prevented.

Grandier is promised a quick death: the executioner promises to tighten a noose around his neck before the fire reaches him. As the flames rise, one of Grandier's tormentors is forced by the citizens to give the kiss of peace; but in a final act of treachery, he knots the noose rope, rendering it useless. The dying Grandier sees the townspeople having a celebration as de Laubardemont begins demolishing the town walls.

When it is over, the cynical de Laubardemont visits Jeanne for the last time, leaving her with dreary images of the bore-dom in store for her now that her devils are gone. He pre-sents her with a grisly relic--Grandier's charred thigh-bone. Madeleine, who has been imprisoned all this time, emerges as her husband's ashes are being scattered to the four winds; she picks her way over the rubble of the walls and walks down the road away from Loudun.

Credits:

Director:	Ken Russell
Producers:	Robert H. Solo and Ken Russell (Russo Productions/Warner Brothers)
Associate Producer:	Roy Baird
Screenplay:	Ken Russell, based on the play by John Whiting and the book The Devils of Loudun by Aldous Huxley
Photography:	David Watkin (Panavision; color by Technicolor)
Cameraman:	Ronnie Taylor
Assistant Cameraman:	Peter Ewens
Lighting:	John Swan
Sound:	Brian Simmons and Terry Rawlings
Original Music:	Composed and conducted by Peter Maxwell Davies; performed by The Fires of London
Period Music:	Arranged and conducted by David Munrow; performed by The Early Music Consort of London
Art Director:	Robert Cartwright
Assistant Art Director:	Alan Tomkins
Set Designer:	Derek Jarman
Set Decorator:	Ian Whittaker
Property Master:	George Ball
Construction:	Terry Apsey
Editor:	Michael Bradsell
Assistant Editor:	Stuart Baird
Choreographer:	Terry Gilbert
Production Manager:	Neville C. Thompson
Assistant Director:	Ted Morley
Unit Manager:	Graham Ford
Makeup:	Charles Parker
Hairstyles:	Ramon Gow
Costumes:	Shirley Russell
Wardrobe Supervisor:	Tiny Nicholls
Cast:	Oliver Reed (Urbain Grandier), Vanessa Redgrave (Sister Jeanne des Anges), Dudley Sutton (Baron de Laubardemont), Max Adrian (Ibert), Gemma Jones (Madeleine de Brou), Murray Melvin (Mignon), Michael Gothard (Father Barré), Georgina Hale (Phillipe Trinçant), Brian Murphy (Adam), Christopher Logue (Cardinal Richelieu), Graham Armitage (Louis XIII), John Woodvine (Trinçant), Andrew Faulds (Rangier), Kenneth Colley (Legrand), Judith Paris (Sister Judith), Catherine Wilmer (Sister Catherine), Iza

                          Teller [Izabella Telezynska] (Sister
                          Iza), James Mellor (Executioner),
                          Oliver MacGreevy (Helper), Maggy
                          Maxwell (Madame de Brou), Lawrence
                          Trimble (Dream Grandier), Jonathan
                          Kramer (Duc de Condé), James, Xavier,
                          and Alexander Russell (Court chil-
                          dren)

Filmed at Pinewood
Studios, England.
Distribution: Warner Brothers
Running time: 111 minutes (9,990 feet)
Released: 16 July 1971 (New York City)

6   THE BOY FRIEND (Great Britain, 1971)

     Seedy director Max Mandeville's tacky repertory company is
performing The Boy Friend at an even tackier provincial playhouse. When his star, Rita, injures her leg Max calls upon his
shy assistant stage manager, Polly Browne, to take her place.
Polly's insecurity is increased by the fact that she is madly
and, she thinks, hopelessly in love with Tony, the leading
man. Rita rather superciliously coaches her uncertain efforts
at song-and-dance; luckily the rest of the cast is on her side
--for the moment anyway.
     The performance doesn't begin smoothly--Polly's first scene
is, to put it kindly, tentatively acted. The cast has found
out that big-time movie director De Thrill is in the audience
(he very nearly is the audience), thinking of filming the play
and scouting for new talent to bring back to Hollywood. The
members of the cast set out to upstage one another in a bid
for De Thrill's attention, which hampers Polly further. And
every time she looks at Tony, he seems to be having a tête-à-
tête with a flashy chorine.
     The play concerns a rich girl and boy, Polly and Tony, who
meet in France. Since neither of them can be sure whether
people like them for themselves or their money, each is living
incognito. She attends a finishing school and he works as a
bell-boy. Thinking each other poor, they fall in love but
fear telling the truth about themselves. After some misunder-
standings the facts are revealed and the lovers are united.
As De Thrill watches the rather sleazy production, he imagines
how his film will be--a glittery Busby Berkeley style extravaganza. He sees Tony and Polly (who has become more sure of
herself with Tony's support) doing Astaire-Rogers routines in
white tie, tails and silver lamé on fantastic Art Deco sets.
     The play ends. Polly is astonished when Tony declares his
love for her. Maisie, one of the chorines, who has fancied
that De Thrill is interested in her, experiences a disappoint-
ment when she finds out his attention has really been for her

tall, talented partner, Tommy--who, it turns out, is De Thrill's long-lost son. De Thrill and the boy leave; the film-maker has decided not to film The Boy Friend, saying he prefers to do Singin' in the Rain. He leaves a note for Polly inviting her to Hollywood. Tony is afraid she would rather become a star than stay with him in England, but she convinces him he's mistaken.

Songs: "The Boy Friend," "I Could Be Happy With You," "Perfect Young Ladies," "Won't You Charleston With Me?," "Fancy Forgetting," "Sur La Plage," "A Room in Bloomsbury," "Safety in Numbers," "It's Never Too Late to Fall in Love," "Poor Little Pierrette," "Riviera," "The You-Don't-Want-to-Play-With-Me Blues," "All I Do Is Dream of You," "You Are My Lucky Star," "Any Old Iron."

Credits:

Director:	Ken Russell
Producer:	Ken Russell (Russflix, Ltd., an EMI-MGM Presentation)
Associate Producer:	Harry Benn
Production Associate:	Justin de Villeneuve
Screenplay:	Ken Russell, from the musical play by Sandy Wilson
Photography:	David Watkin (Panavision; color by Metrocolor)
Cameraman:	Alan McCabe
Assistant Cameraman:	Peter Ewens
Sound Editor:	Don Challis
Sound Recorders:	Brian Simmons, Maurice Askew
Music/Songs:	Sandy Wilson "All I Do Is Dream of You" and "You Are My Lucky Star" by Nacio Herb Brown and Arthur Freed "Any Old Iron" by Charles Collins, E. A. Sheppard, and Fred Terry
Musical Director:	Peter Maxwell Davies
Pianist:	Peter Greenwell
Production Designer:	Tony Walton
Art Director:	Simon Holland
Set Decorator:	Ian Whittaker
Construction:	Charles Hammelton
Editor:	Michael Bradsell
Choreographers:	Christopher Gable, Gillian Gregory, Terry Gilbert, and members of the cast
Production Manager:	Neville C. Thompson
Assistant Director:	Graham Ford
Chief Makeup:	Freddie Williamson
Chief Hairstylist:	Barbara Ritchie

Property Master:	George Ball
Costumes:	Shirley Russell
Wardrobe Supervisor:	John Brady
Film Research:	Philip Jenkinson
Cast:	Twiggy (Polly Browne), Christopher Gable (Tony Brockhurst), Barbara Windsor (Hortense), Moyra Fraser (Mme. Dubonnet/Mrs. Parkhill), Bryan Pringle (Percival Browne/Mr. Percy Parkhill), Max Adrian (Lord Brockhurst/Max Mandeville), Catherine Wilmer (Lady Brockhurst/Catherine), Vladek Sheybal (De Thrill), Anne Jameson ("Mrs. Peter"), Peter Greenwell (Pianist), Glenda Jackson (Rita), Antonia Ellis (Maisie), Caryl Little (Dulcie), Georgina Hale (Fay), Sally Bryant (Nancy), Tommy Tune (Tommy), Murray Melvin (Alphonse), Graham Armitage (Michael), Brian Murphy (Peter), Robert La Bassier (Chauffeur)
Filmed on location at Theatre Royal, Portsmouth; fantasy sequences at the EMI-MGM Elstree Studios.	
Distribution:	Metro-Goldwyn-Mayer/EMI
Running time:	123 minutes (11,250 feet)
Released:	16 December 1971 (New York City)

7   SAVAGE MESSIAH (Great Britain, 1972)

The year is 1910. Henri Gaudier, an impoverished 18-year-old art student in Paris, meets Sophie Brzeska, a 38-year-old Polish would-be novelist. As they stroll through Luxembourg Gardens, his very visceral attitude toward life and art clashes with her spiritual one. However, they are both alone and alienated, and are drawn together. Sophie refuses to become his mistress or to marry him, having an abhorrence of sex, but they take lodgings together in a squalid little hole in London, living as brother and sister and adopting the surname Gaudier-Brzeska. Henri takes a job as a construction worker and Sophie begs on the street. After a long period of non-success, Henri is befriended by an art dealer, Angus Corky, who introduces him to another dealer, Lionel Shaw.

Shaw expresses an interest in seeing the new sculpture that Henri has been talking about and appoints to come to his studio the next morning. Henri has no sculpture done; in fact

he hasn't even a slab of stone to work on. With the help of
Sophie and Corky he pilfers a gravestone and sculpts all night,
expounding his theories of life and art all the while. When
Shaw doesn't come, Henri hurls the completed sculpture through
Shaw's gallery window.

Fed up with Henri's impulsiveness and ill-temper, Sophie
takes a governess' post in Dorset. Henri takes up with Gosh
Smith-Boyle, a young suffragette. Corky arranges an exhibition of Henri's work and, armed with this good news, Henri
visits Sophie and they celebrate. She vaguely promises to
marry him soon. Later, returning to London, Sophie finds Gosh
in Henri's room and angrily withdraws to get her own lodgings,
where she works on the catalogue for the exhibition.

World War I breaks out. Henri avoids enlisting for the
sake of his art, and Gosh, who fancies herself a patriot,
leaves him in contempt. Finally, outraged and dismayed by
the destruction of Rheims Cathedral, and disheartened by
Sophie's continued rejection of marriage, Henri enters the
army. He is killed in action at the age of 23, leaving the
grief-stricken Sophie to manage his now-posthumous exhibition.

Credits:

Director:	Ken Russell
Producer:	Ken Russell (A Russ-Arts Ltd. Production for M-G-M)
Associate Producer:	Harry Benn
Production Associates:	John and Benny Lee
Screenplay:	Christopher Logue, based on the book by H. S. Ede
Photography:	Dick Bush (Metrocolor)
Cameraman:	Ronnie Taylor
Assistant Cameraman:	Eddie Collins
Sound Editor:	Stuart Baird
Sound Recorder:	Robin Gregory
Sound Re-recorder:	Doug Turner
Original Music:	Michael Garret
Additional Music:	"Nuages" and "Sirenes" by Claude Debussy, from the Nocturnes Song, "Two Fleas," written and sung by Dorothy Tutin
Production Designer:	Derek Jarman
Art Director:	George Lack
Set Decorator:	Ian Whittaker
Property Master:	George Ball
Editor:	Michael Bradsell
Artist:	Paul Dufficey
Production Manager:	Neville C. Thompson
Assistant Director:	Graham Ford
Makeup:	Freddie Williamson

Hairstyles:	Betty Glasgow
Costumes:	Shirley Russell
Wardrobe Supervisor:	Tiny Nicholls
Cast:	Dorothy Tutin (Sophie Brzeska, Scott Antony (Henri Gaudier), Helen Mirren (Gosh Smith-Boyle), Lindsay Kemp (Angus Corky), Michael Gough (M. Gaudier), John Justin (Lionel Shaw), Aubrey Richards (Mayor), Peter Vaughan (Museum Attendant), Ben Aris (Thomas Buff), Eleanor Fazan (Mme. Gaudier), Otto Diamant (Mr. Saltzman), Susanna East (Pippa), Maggy Maxwell (Tart), Imogen Claire (Mavis Coldstream), Judith Paris (Kate), Robert Lang (Major Boyle), Alex Jawdokimov (Library student), Paul McDowell (Agitator), Claire Marshall (Maid), Howard Goorney and Henry Woolf (Gendarmes)
Filmed on location in England at Bath, Bristol, Weymouth, and Arundel. Interiors filmed at Lee International Studios, London.	
Distribution:	Metro-Goldwyn-Mayer
Running time:	103 minutes (9,310 feet)
Released:	15 September 1972 (London)

8   MAHLER (Great Britain, 1974)

Gustav Mahler, on a train journey with his wife, reflects on the events of his unhappy life. Alma recalls the incidents leading to their estrangement.

Gustav is frustrated as a child in a large, noisy Jewish family. He dreams of becoming a composer, but his mediocre piano teacher holds him back artistically.

After Mahler breaks into musical circles he marries the younger Alma, herself a budding composer. He is haunted, however, by constant fears that she will be unfaithful, especially with her chief admirer, an insolent soldier named Max. Mahler has extravagant, grotesque fantasies about her supposed infidelity, one of which has her dancing lewdly on a coffin in which he is imprisoned, screaming. He strains their relationship further by belittling her musical talent, ignoring her efforts at composition and setting her to work as his copyist.

Mahler struggles to make a living conducting in order to finance his desire to compose. His brother Otto, an unsuccessful musician himself whom Mahler is supporting, kills himself. Then, as Gustav composes his "Kindertotenlieder" cycle, one of his children dies.

In order to make a living, Mahler wishes to conduct the Vienna orchestra; to do this he must win the favor of the influential, violently anti-Semitic Cosima Wagner. He converts to Christianity and remembers the humiliation in a dream in which, dressed as a Viking and acting like Stan Laurel, he slays a pig and eats its nose for the approval of the leather-and-swastika-clad Cosima.

Driven by his work and his fears that Alma will leave him, Mahler develops a strained heart. This troubles him as he rides the train; he becomes ill and the doctor who attends him diagnoses a mild ailment. Max, who is on the train, asks Alma to leave with him. As the journey ends, however, Gustav reassures her of his love for her, and she stays with him.

But he is more ill than either of them suspect, and his heart fails soon after they disembark.

Credits:

Director:	Ken Russell
Producer:	Roy Baird (Goodtimes Enterprises/Ken Russell)
Executive Producers:	David Puttnam, Sandy Lieberson
Screenplay:	Ken Russell
Photography:	Dick Bush (Technicolor)
Special Effects:	John Richardson
Sound Recorder:	Iain Bruce
Sound Re-recorders:	Ian Fuller, Gerry Humphreys
Music/Songs:	Extracts from Gustav Mahler's Symphonies No. 1-7, 9, 10; played by the Amsterdam Concertgebouw Orchestra, conducted by Bernard Haitink
	Mahler's "Kindertotenlieder" No. 5, sung by Carol Mudie, and No. 3
	Wagner's "Liebestod" from <u>Tristan und Isolde</u>, sung by Carol Mudie
	Wagner's "Ride of the Valkyries" from <u>Die Walkure</u>; lyrics by Ken Russell, sung by Robert Powell and Antonia Ellis
	"Otto's Sunset" by Michael Moores, played by Peter Eyre
	"Alma's Song" by Dana Gillespie and William Black; played by David Rennie, sung by Carol Mudie
Music Coordinator:	John Forsyth
Art Director:	Ian Whittaker
Editor:	Michael Bradsell
Choreographer:	Gillian Gregory

Production Supervisor:	John Comfort
Assistant Director:	Michael Gowans
Costumes:	Shirley Russell
Cast:	Robert Powell (Gustav Mahler), Georgina Hale (Alma Mahler), Richard Morant (Max), Lee Montague (Bernhard Mahler), Rosalie Crutchley (Marie Mahler), Benny Lee (Uncle Arnold), Miriam Karlin (Aunt Rosa), Angela Down (Justine), David Collings (Hugo Wolf), Ronald Pickup (Nick), Antonia Ellis (Cosima Wagner), Kenneth Colley (Krenek), Arnold Yarrow (Grandfather), Dana Gillespie (Anna von Mildenburg), Elaine Delmar (Princess), Michael Southgate (Alois Mahler), Otto Diamant (Professor Sladky), Gary Rich (Young Mahler), Peter Eyre (Otto), George Coulouris (Dr. Roth), Andrew Faulds (Doctor on train), David Trevena (Dr. Richter), Sarah McLellan (Putzi), Claire McLellan (Glucki), Oliver Reed (Conductor)
Filmed on location in England in the Lakes District.	
Distribution:	Visual Programme Systems
Running time:	115 minutes (10,378 feet)
Release:	4 April 1974 (London) (Mahler has not yet gone into general release in the U. S., although it was shown briefly in Los Angeles in early 1975 and again in New York in April 1976.)

9   TOMMY (Great Britain, 1974)

1945. After a brief romantic idyll in the hills with his wife, Nora, Group Captain Walker is called back to duty. During an air raid his plane is shot down in flames and he is presumed dead. Nora is pregnant, though, and their child, Tommy, is born on VE Day. In 1951 Nora takes the boy to Bernie's Holiday Camp, where she receives the attentions of a camp host, the lecherous Frank Hobbs. Realizing how much she wants the male companionship Frank is eager to provide, Nora brings him home after the holiday; they plan to marry. However, the missing Captain Walker soon reappears. He visits Tommy's room, then finds Nora and Frank together in his own. Startled,

Frank kills Walker, then notices that Tommy has witnessed the crime. Nora and Frank insist doggedly, "You didn't see it, you didn't hear it, you won't say nothing to no one...." This renders the boy psychosomatically deaf, dumb, and blind; he becomes totally self-absorbed. Tommy's obliviousness to the traditions surrounding Christmas causes Nora to fear for his spiritual state and to devote herself to finding a cure for his condition.

Even after Tommy has grown up, his mother continues to subject him to various "miracle cures," including a visit to a shrine for worshippers of Marilyn Monroe. Frank, now a shill for a strip joint, turns Tommy over to a prostitute who gives him LSD, promising to "put him right." He is also left alone with his sadistic Cousin Kevin, who tortures him, and his weird Uncle Ernie, who molests him. Each of these experiences changes the image that he sees in the mirror he stands in front of for hours. Stimulated by his new self-image, he wanders off and is found in a junkyard, frantically playing an old pinball machine. Frank sees the possibilities and soon Tommy becomes a pinball champ, enabling his parents to live in flashy nouveau-riche splendor. On the day of the big pinball championship Nora, full of champagne and guilt about her ambivalent feelings about her son, smashes the TV screen on which she can see only commercials and Tommy's face. In her delirium, she hallucinates that she is wallowing erotically in baked beans, soapsuds, and melted chocolate.

Frank finds a doctor, a Harley Street smoothie who, after running some spurious tests and accepting a large check, can only opine that Tommy's illness is mental, as he makes bedroom eyes at Nora. Returning home, the frustrated Nora pushes Tommy through a mirror and into the ocean outside. This breaks the spell; Tommy swims and runs, exhilarated by his freedom. By the time Nora finds him he has come to know that his self-realization is a result of sensory deprivation and pinball. He founds a new religion based on these elements and opens his home to his followers. The home proves too small, so Tommy builds his own Holiday Camp. Soon his religion is a going concern, complete with all the trappings his opportunistic relatives can think up, and his parents are rich beyond even Frank's wildest dreams. But when Tommy starts preaching his gospel of inner-direction, his followers, who have been mercilessly cheated, rebel. They destroy the camp and kill Nora and Frank. Tommy escapes and flees into the country, finally arriving at the place of his conception in the hills.

Songs: "Prologue--1945," "Captain Walker/It's a Boy," "Bernie's Holiday Camp," "1951/What About the Boy?," "Amazing Journey," "Christmas," "Eyesight to the Blind," "Acid Queen," "Do You Think It's Alright (Nos. 1, 2, and 3)," "Cousin Kevin,"

"Fiddle About," "Sparks," "Extra, Extra, Extra," "Pinball Wizard," "Champagne," "There's a Doctor," "Go to the Mirror," "Tommy Can You Hear Me?" "Smash the Mirror," "I'm Free," "Mother and Son," "Sensation," "Miracle Cure," "Sally Simpson," "Welcome," "T.V. Studio," "Tommy's Holiday Camp," "We're Not Gonna Take It," "Listening to You/See Me, Feel Me."

Credits:

Director:	Ken Russell
Producers:	Robert Stigwood, Ken Russell
Executive Producers:	Beryl Vertue, Christopher Stamp
Associate Producer:	Harry Benn
Screenplay:	Ken Russell, based on the rock opera by Pete Townshend and the Who; additional material by John Entwistle, Keith Moon
Photography:	Dick Bush, Ronnie Taylor (Eastmancolor)
Special Effects:	Effects Associates, Nobby Clarke, Camera Effects; special photo effects by Robin Lehman
Sound Recorder:	Iain Bruce
Sound Re-recorder:	Bill Rowe
Quintaphonic Sound:	Developed by John Mosley
Music/Songs:	Pete Townshend "Fiddle About" and "Cousin Kevin" by John Entwistle "Eyesight to the Blind" by Sonny Boy Williamson "Tommy's Holiday Camp" by Keith Moon
Music Director:	Pete Townshend
Musicians:	Elton John, Eric Clapton, Keith Moon, John Entwistle, Ronnie Wood, Kenny Jones, Nicky Hopkins, Chris Stainton, Fuzzy Samuels, Caleb Quaye, Mick Ralphs, Graham Deakin, Phil Chen, Alan Ross, Richard Bailey, Dave Clinton, Tony Newman, Mike Kelly, Dee Murray, Nigel Olsson, Ray Cooper, Davey Johnstone, Geoff Daley, Bob Efford, Ronnie Ross, Howie Casey Music synthesizer programmer: Pete Townshend Theatre organ played by Gerald Shaw; arranged by Martyn Ford
Vocal Chorus:	Liza Strike, Simon Townshend, Mylon Le Fevre, Billy Nicholls, Jeff Roden, Margo Newman, Gillian McIntosh, Vicki Brown, Kit Trevor, Helen Shappell, Paul Gurvitz, Alison Dowling

Art Director: John Clark
Set Decorator: Paul Dufficey, Ian Whittaker
Editor: Stuart Baird
Choreography: Gillian Gregory
Production Manager: John Comfort
Assistant Director: Jonathan Benson
Makeup: George Blackler, Peter Robb-King
Costumes: Shirley Russell
Cast: Ann-Margret (Nora Walker Hobbs),
                         Oliver Reed (Frank Hobbs), Roger
                         Daltrey (Tommy), Elton John (Pinball
                         Wizard), Eric Clapton (Preacher),
                         Keith Moon (Uncle Ernie), Jack
                         Nicholson (Doctor), Robert Powell
                         (Group Captain Walker), Paul Nicho-
                         las (Cousin Kevin), Tina Turner
                         (Acid Queen), Barry Winch (Young
                         Tommy), Victoria Russell (Sally Simp-
                         son), Ben Aris (Reverend Simpson),
                         Mary Holland (Mrs. Simpson), Jenni-
                         fer and Susan Baker (Nurses), Juliet
                         and Gillian King (Handmaidens to
                         Acid Queen), Imogen Claire (Nurse),
                         John Entwistle and Pete Townshend
                         (Themselves), Arthur Brown (Priest),
                         Gary Rich (Rock musician), Dick
                         Allan (President of Black Angels),
                         Eddie Stacey (Bovver Boy)
Distribution: Columbia
Running time: 108 minutes (9,755 feet)
Released: 19 March 1975 (New York City)

10   LISZTOMANIA (Great Britain, 1975)

In a fantasy sequence, Franz Liszt makes love to his mistress, Marie d'Agoult, inside a piano, in time to a metronome
whose tempo Marie keeps increasing. They are discovered by
her foppish husband, the Count d'Agoult. Marie eats a banana
as she watches d'Agoult chase the scantily-clad Liszt around
the room with a sword. The Count nails the lovers inside a
piano-coffin and puts it on the railroad tracks.

At a party teeming with musical luminaries, the struggling
composer Richard Wagner asks the superstar Liszt to play some
of his music at a concert. Liszt does so, but, to Wagner's
dismay and humiliation, the nineteenth-century teenyboppers
in the audience only want to hear Liszt play his big hit,
"Chopsticks."

Another fantasy shows the decline of Liszt's relationship
with Marie in a Chaplinesque silent movie in which the lovers
become more and more bored.

Liszt, leaving his daughter Cosima to marry his friend Hans von Bulow, goes to Russia and accepts the overtures of Princess Carolyn, wife of the insane Tsar Nicholas. The jilted Marie writes a scathing pamphlet about Liszt called Lisztomania.

In yet another fantasy, Liszt sports a giant phallus. The women in his life dance on and around the huge member. Carolyn castrates him and he finds himself pulled into a giant vagina.

Wagner, meanwhile, has formed an acquaintance with Liszt. Wagner is seen drugging Liszt's wine and sucking his blood, just as he drains off Liszt's musical genius in order to augment his own talent.

The affair with Carolyn over, Liszt becomes a priest, albeit a non-celibate one. He receives a surprise visit from the Pope while naked in bed with his copyist, Olga Janine. He tries to pass her off as a male assistant despite the fact that she won't stay under the blankets. The Pope orders him to exorcise Wagner, who, through his Fascist philosophy and music, has become the Antichrist.

Liszt travels to Wagner's spooky old castle. Wagner has destroyed von Bulow and married Cosima; together they perform half-pagan Fascist rites for an audience of rapt onlookers. Wagner shows Liszt his Superman, a giant gold-plated golem. When activated the thing mutters "Stein, stein." Wagner takes this to be part of a Jewish name and thus the desired expression of anti-Semitism. The golem, however, only wants a stein of beer. As it drinks, belches and urinates in the fireplace, Wagner realizes that his creation is a dud and returns to the drawing board.

Liszt begins to play his own music and, in so doing, brings the castle down around Wagner. He, however, is trapped and slowly killed through the voodooish activities of the spiteful Cosima, as he watches Wagner rise from his grave reincarnated as Hitler.

In Heaven, Liszt and his ladies (Marie, Cosima, Olga, Carolyn and some casual encounters), all reconciled, enter a celestial rocket ship shaped like a gigantic pipe organ and pilot it to Earth. Liszt uses a ray gun to destroy Wagner-Hitler. The ship soars back into Heaven as Liszt sings "Peace at last."

Credits:

Director:	Ken Russell
Producers:	Roy Baird, David Puttnam (Visual Programme Systems/Goodtimes Enterprises)
Executive Producer:	Sandy Lieberson
Screenplay:	Ken Russell
Photography:	Peter Suschitsky (Panavision)
Special Effects:	Colin Chilvers, Roy Spencer

Sound Editor:	Terry Rawlings
Sound Recorder:	Iain Bruce
Sound Re-recorder:	Bill Rowe
Music/Songs:	Composed by Rick Wakeman, incorporating themes from the work of Franz Liszt and Richard Wagner. Lyrics by Jonathan Benson, Roger Daltrey, Ken Russell. Performed by The English Rock Ensemble, The National Philharmonic Orchestra
Music Coordinator:	John Forsyth
Solo Vocalists:	Roger Daltrey, Paul Nicholas, Linda Lewis, Mandy Moore
Instrumental Soloists:	David Wilde (piano), William Davies (organ), Jack Bruce (bass guitar)
Art Director:	Philip Harrison
Set Decorator:	Ian Whittaker
Editor:	Stuart Baird
Titles and Opticals:	Stewart Hardy Films
Choreographer:	Imogen Claire
Fencing Master:	Peter Brayham
Production Manager:	Peter Price
Assistant Directors:	Jonathan Benson, Terry Needham
Makeup:	Wally Schneiderman
Costumes:	Shirley Russell
Cast:	Roger Daltrey (Franz Liszt), Sara Kestelman (Princess Carolyn), Paul Nicholas (Richard Wagner), Fiona Lewis (Marie d'Agoult), Veronica Quilligan (Cosima), Nell Campbell (Olga Janine), John Justin (Count d'Agoult), Ringo Starr (Pope), Andrew Reilly (Hans von Bulow), Anulka Dziubinska (Lola Montes), Imogen Claire (George Sand), David English (Captain of Hussars), Peter Brayham (Liszt's bodyguard), Rick Wakeman (Thor/Siegfried), Rikki Howard (Countess), Felicity Devonshire (Governess), Aubrey Morris (Opera house manager), Kenneth Colley (Chopin), Ken Parry (Rossini), Otto Diamant (Mendelssohn), Murray Melvin (Berlioz), Andrew Faulds (Richard Strauss), Oliver Reed (Carolyn's servant), Georgina Hale (Lady at concert)
Filmed at Shepperton Studios, England. Distribution:	Columbia/Warner

Running time: 104 minutes (9,351 feet)
Released: 10 October 1975 (New York City)

11   VALENTINO (Great Britain, 1977)

During the riots following Rudolph Valentino's death, several boorish newspapermen corner the women in his life. One of the first is Bianca de Saulles, widow of an influential gangster, who denies that he was a "pansy" and a gigolo. She had taken private lessons from him when he was a professional partner in a dance hall. The fact that he used the hall's facilities for these lessons roused the ire of its owner, Billie.

In a flashback, Billie calls Bianca's husband, with whom she is intimate, and tells him about the private lessons. He comes to the dance hall that evening, insults Valentino, and drags Bianca away. Billie fires Rudy.

Later, Rudolph catches, and photographs, Billie in bed with de Saulles, giving Bianca grounds to leave him. She does, but some of his henchmen attack her, her son, and Rudy at his apartment, and force her to return with them. She later kills her husband.

Another mourner is June Mathis, Rudy's mentor and friend during his early career. She recalls her first glimpse of him as partner to a drunken exhibition dancer in southern California. Fatty Arbuckle is in the audience and humiliates the woman; Valentino, in retaliation, dances obscenely with Fatty's girl, a dumb starlet. He goes home with her to her opulent house, which she has gotten after just a year in films. She tells him he should try acting.

He does, making a two-reel comedy as a dancing gigolo. June tries to tell the studio heads that he would make a terrific Latin lover type, but they are dubious, especially because Rudy's wife had left him on their wedding night.

A spectacular entrance is made by another mourner, Alla Nazimova, Valentino's first leading lady. She launches, without prompting, on her reminiscence. She sees a film of Valentino in The Four Horsemen of the Apocalypse and decides he must be Armand in her production of Camille. After doing this film, the lesbian Nazimova, her "protegée" designer Natasha Rambova, and Rudy begin to plan a film on the history of dance, and, in preparation, take a series of slightly outré photographs. Nazimova, jealous of the growing attraction between Rudy and Rambova, releases some of the photos to the press, exposing Valentino to ridicule and criticism.

Rambova also appears at the funeral and tells her story: she and Rudy leave Nazimova and marry in Mexico, although he is still married. When they return to California, they are put in jail. Her bail is $500, which is put up by her stepfather, cosmetic tycoon Richard Hudnut. His is $10,000, which

Jesse Lasky, the studio head, refuses to put up because it means free publicity. The faithful June gets the money together, but not before Valentino spends a humiliating, horrifying night in jail.

The charges are dropped, since Mexican marriages aren't recognized in California, and Rudy and Rambova walk out on Lasky. Rudy can't work as an actor for two years, the duration of his contract with Lasky, but George Ullman, a small-time entrepreneur working for a cosmetics company, has another idea. He approaches them, as they live in blissful poverty, with an idea for an evening of interpretive dance sponsored by his company. They agree and are wildly successful. Lasky engineers their return to his studio, with Rambova as an artistic advisor.

During the filming of <u>Monsieur Beaucaire</u>, someone implies that Valentino is a "pink powder puff" who is sissifying the American male. Soon the contract with Lasky expires, and Rudy goes to United Artists. Rambova, however, is forbidden on the lot. They separate, and she makes a terrible, bitter film, <u>What Price Beauty</u>?, which does a hatchet job on Valentino.

The "powder puff" remark gets into the press in a scathing editorial on Valentino's effect on American manhood. He challenges the author to a fight; a beefy ex-Navy boxer, Rory O'Neil, accepts on behalf of the press.

The affair of honor deteriorates into a field day for the press. Rudy fares badly in the first two rounds, as his friends George and June beg him to stop the fight. After being stunned and humiliated by O'Neil, Valentino comes back in the third round to win.

O'Neil challenges him to a drinking bout. Despite an ulcer which has been troubling him, Rudy accepts, and eventually drinks his opponent under the table. He goes home, roaring drunk, and suffers an ulcer attack which ultimately kills him.

<u>Credits</u>:

Director:	Ken Russell
Producers:	Irvin Winkler, Robert Chartoff (Chartoff-Winkler Productions)
Executive Producer:	Robert Chartoff
Associate Producer:	Harry Benn
Screenplay:	Mardik Martin and Ken Russell; based on <u>Valentino: An Intimate Exposé of the Sheik</u> by Brad Steiger and Chaw Mank
Photography:	Peter Suschitsky (Panavision; color by Deluxe)
Cameramen:	Ronnie Taylor, Kelvin Pike
Sound Recorder:	John Mitchell
Music:	Composed by Ferde Grofé and Stanley Black; performed by the National Philharmonic Orchestra

Musical Director:	Stanley Black
Art Director:	Philip Harrison
Set Decorator:	Ian Whittaker
Property Master:	Ray Traynor
Construction:	Jeffrey Woodbridge
Editor:	Stuart Baird
Choreographer:	Gillian Gregory
Production Manager:	Peter Price
Location Manager:	Richard Green
Assistant Director:	Jonathan Benson
Production Accountant:	Len Cave
Production Secretary:	Pat Pennelegion
Continuity:	Zelda Barron
Casting:	Maude Spector
Make-up:	Peter Robb-King
Hairdresser:	Colin Jamison
Costumes:	Shirley Russell
Wardrobe Master:	Richard Pointing
Wardrobe Mistress:	Rebecca Breed
Dialog Coach:	Marcella Markham
Stills Photographer:	Barry Peake
Publicist:	Brian Doyle
Cast:	Rudolf Nureyev (Rudolph Valentino), Leslie Caron (Alla Nazimova), Michelle Phillips (Natasha Rambova), Carol Kane (Fatty's Girl), Felicity Kendal (June Mathis), Seymour Cassell (George Ullman), Huntz Hall (Jesse Lasky), Alfred Marks (Richard Rowland), David De Keyser (Joseph Schenck), Linda Thorson (Billie Streeter), Leland Palmer (Marjorie Tain), Lindsay Kemp (Angus McBride), Peter Vaughan (Rory O'Neil), Anthony Dowell (Vaslav Nijinsky), Penelope Milford (Lorna Sinclair), June Bolton (Bianca de Saulles), Robin Clark (Jack de Saulles), William Hootkins (Fatty), John Justin (Sidney Olcott), Anton Diffring (Baron Long), Nicolette Marvin (Marsha Lee), Jennie Linden (Agnes Ayres), Percy Herbert (Studio guard), Dudley Sutton (Willie), Christine Carlson (Girl in tango sequence), Don Fellows (George Melford), Bill McKinney (Policeman), Marcella Markham (Hooker), John Alderson (Cop), Elizabeth Bagley (Pretty girl), Charles Farrell (Drunk), Hal Galili (Harry Fischbeck), Richard Le Parmentier (The

Sheik), Scott Miller (Ray C. Smallwood), Burnell Tucker (Assistant
Director), Diana Von Fossen (Make-up
girl), Ray Jewers (Electrician),
Murray Salem (Vagrant), Mildred Shay
(Lady at Maxim's), Deirdre Costello
(First whore), Diana Weston (Second
whore), Mark Baker (Assistant Director), Amy Farber (Girl friend)

Filmed at EMI Elstree
Studios, Borehamwood,
England and on location.
Distribution: United Artists
Running time: 127 minutes

Writings about Ken Russell, 1964-1977

1964

12 ANON. "When Talent is Not Enough." The Times [London] (21
    May), p. 16.
        French Dressing fails despite the promise shown by those
    involved, due to simple unfunniness, poor timing, and Rus-
    sell's lack of a "gift for directing actors."

13 COLEMAN, JOHN. "Last Resort." New Statesman, 67 (29 May),
    854.
        French Dressing has a "peculiar charm and freshness."
    The visual gags are almost too plentiful, but many are
    effective.

14 EYLES, ALLEN. "French Dressing." Films and Filming, 10
    (July), 24-25.
        Tired plot becomes an "enjoyable spree" at Russell's
    hands but it is ultimately "superficial" satire, "bashing
    at the same old inoffensive targets."

15 MALLETT, RICHARD. Review of French Dressing. Punch, 246 (3
    June), 834.
        Film wastes ideas and people. Its humor is predominant-
    ly indiscriminate and ill-timed.

16 S., A. "French Dressing." [BFI] Monthly Film Bulletin, 31
    (June), 88-89.
        Credits, synopsis, short review which calls film a
    "spirited endeavor" on Russell's part which accomplishes
    little. The pace and timing are poor, familiar devices
    are overworked. Russell has "a limited flair with actors."

1967

17 ANON. "Billion Dollar Brain." Films and Filming, 14 (Decem-
    ber), 48.
        Photo preview.

1967

18   COLEMAN, JOHN.   Review of Billion Dollar Brain.   New Statesman,
        74 (17 November), 690.
            Notice says "film looks better than its script" and is
        a waste of money and Russell's talent.

19   CROWTHER, BOSLEY.   "Billion Dollar Brain."   New York Times
        (23 December), p. 29.
            The Harry Palmer character is "eclipsed" and nearly
        buried by the scenery and the vagaries of the plot.

20   DENT, ALAN.   Review of Billion Dollar Brain.   Illustrated
        London News, 252 (25 November), 32.
            Notice finds plot and motivation hopelessly muddled.

*21 LANGLEY, LEE.   "The Einstein File."   Guardian [Manchester]
        (26 October), p. 6.
            Probably concerns Billion Dollar Brain.   [Cited in
        British Humanities Index 1967, p. 387.]

22   MALLETT, RICHARD.   Review of Billion Dollar Brain.   Punch,
        253 (22 November), 792-93.
            Although the script is weak, once one's sympathy has
        been engaged the film is entertaining and visually
        interesting.

23   OTTA.   "Billion Dollar Brain."   Variety, 249 (22 November),
        6.
            Film is slow-starting and hard to follow.   Russell pro-
        vides speed but no transitions.

                                1968

24   ALPERT, HOLLIS.   Review of Billion Dollar Brain.   Saturday
        Review, 51 (6 January), 38.
            In this film, Harry Palmer has lost his uniqueness and
        gained too much gadgetry.

25   ANON.   "Billion Dollar Brain."   Filmfacts, 10 (15 January),
        413-14.
            Credits, synopsis, and excerpts from popular-press
        reviews.

26   ANON.   "Billion Dollar Brain."   Time, 91 (5 January), 74.
            As the third Harry Palmer film, it suffers due to the
        law of diminishing returns, becoming even more mechanical
        than usual for this kind of film.

27   ANON.   Review of Billion Dollar Brain.   Playboy, 15 (March),
        26.
            Russell "fails to do justice" to the Deighton novel.

28   B., A. N. "Billion Dollar Brain." Christian Science Monitor
      [Eastern edition], 60 (26 February), 4.
          Review.

29   BRAUCOURT, GUY. "Un Cerveau d'Un Milliard de Dollars." Ciné-
      ma, No. 131 (December), pp. 138-39.
          Notice considers the film less successful as a spy
      story than it is as a portrait of American fascism. In
      French.

30   DAVIS, RICHARD. "Billion Dollar Brain." Films and Filming,
      14 (January), 24.
          Although Russell is "one of the few genuine stylists"
      of the British cinema, the story is ill-suited to him;
      he needs a bigger hero, one who lends himself better to
      tongue-in-cheek than Palmer.

31   McMAHAN, IDA and ETHEL WHITEHORN. "Billion Dollar Brain."
      PTA Magazine, 62 (March), 36.
          Notice summarizes film as "not so good."

32   MORGENSTERN, JOSEPH. "Blue Germs." Newsweek, 71 (15 January),
      76, 78.
          Notice points out lack of any real suspense in Billion
      Dollar Brain, although the varied locations add some
      interest.

33   O'SHEY, COMPTROLLER LUDWIG OF THE ARMENIAN PEOPLE'S REPUBLIC.
      "[The] Billion Dollar Brain." Teaspoon and Door [San
      Diego], 1 (24 May), 9.
          The James Bondian element undercuts the cynicism that
      characterized the earlier films.

34   RIPP, JUDITH. "Billion Dollar Brain." Parents' Magazine,
      43 (January), 8, 26.
          Notice calls plot "absurd," going for spoof rather
      than thrills.

35   RONAN, MARGARET. "Billion Dollar Brain." Senior Scholastic,
      91 (11 January), 19.
          Palmer's adventures are unsuitably Bondian.

36   TAYLOR, JOHN RUSSELL. "Billion Dollar Brain." [BFI] Monthly
      Film Bulletin, 35 (January), 2-3.
          Credits, synopsis, review which says that from a "hope-
      ful" beginning, the film deteriorates due to bad pacing
      and generally faulty direction.

37   WALSH, MOIRA. "Three New Films." America, 118 (13 January),
      48.
          Notice calls Billion Dollar Brain politically and mor-
      ally offensive.

1969

38   ANON. "Women in Love." Films and Filming, 16 (December),
        10-11.
            Photo preview.

39   BILLINGTON, MICHAEL. "With Lawrence in Derbyshire." Illus-
        trated London News, 255 (22 November), 24.
            In Women in Love, Russell has done better than expected
        at transposing the difficult, flawed novel. The film errs
        most when trying to be most literal. It is best in its
        evocation of period and in the way Russell plays a scene's
        emotional content off its physical location. He also has
        a talent for good casting.

40   CHRISTIE, IAN LESLIE. "Women in Love." Sight and Sound, 39
        (Winter 1969/70), 49-50.
            In his TV biopics, Russell was able to place his subject
        variously in relation to the viewer--first, in historical
        perspective, and then, subjectively and personally--coup-
        ling basic period evocation with either cinéma vérité or
        tableau or pageant forms. He has not so much adapted
        Women in Love as made a film about it. The film "stands
        or falls as a structure of sharply individualized sequences
        exploiting the range of Russell's ability to convey his
        meaning in purely cinematic terms." This works well in
        his evocation of the Birkin-Crich relationship, but fails
        elsewhere, notable during the "ballet" and some gimmicky
        shots.

41   COLEMAN, JOHN. "Writing It Again." New Statesman, 78 (14
        November), 704.
            In principle, Lawrence scholar F. R. Leavis is correct
        in saying that to film Lawrence is an "obscene undertaking"
        --but there is both splendor and error in the film of
        Women in Love, just as there is in the novel. Among the
        glories is Glenda Jackson and Russell's handling of her
        scenes.

42   COMBS, RICHARD. "Women in Love." [BFI] Monthly Film Bulle-
        tin, 36 (December), 263-64.
            Credits, synopsis, review which praises the lush evo-
        cation of "place," and Russell's careful casting to the
        spirit, rather than the letter, of the novel. However,
        Lawrence's polemics seem sometimes "trivialized" by the
        "pretty" settings.

43   MALLETT, RICHARD. Review of Women in Love. Punch, 257 (19
        November), 842-43.
            Film "isn't satisfactory"; some characters, particu-
        larly Hermione Roddice, and some situations are "hoked up."

The film has too much music; it fails to involve emotionally and to present rounded characters. Its best moments
are "small-scale quiet scenes."

44   RHODE, ERIC. "Chumship." Listener, 82 (20 November), 713.
       Women in Love's very understandability shows its failure
to capture the original. The screenplay misses Lawrence's
point, and Russell is too style-conscious; however, the
film "crackles with its own vitality," and Russell brings
off several odd scenes well.

45   RICH. "Women in Love." Variety, 257 (19 November), 14.
       Film is "episodic but challenging and holding," with a
good cast and production staff. Lawrence's ideas are
"shrewdly put over."

1970

46   ANON. "Futures, Great." Vogue, 156 (July), 92-93.
       Short profile of Russell.

47   ANON. "The Lonely Heart." Films and Filming, 16 (July),
13-16.
       Photo preview of The Music Lovers, under its working
title.

48   ANON. "Quartet of Soloists." Time, 95 (13 April), 103, 106,
109.
       Review of Women in Love.

49   ANON. Review of Women in Love. Playboy, 17 (April), 38.
       Film is surprisingly unverbose, given all the discussions
of love, friendship, etc., within it. Lawrence's ideas
remain powerful in this film, which is created with keen
intelligence, integrity, and meticulous period flavor.

50   ARMSTRONG, MARION. "Spirited Creatures." Christian Century,
87 (16 September), 1099.
       Women in Love is "strongly directed."

51   BLANCHARD, MARGARET. "Men in Charge." Women, 2 (Fall),
31-32.
       Feminist review of Women in Love: "The women exist mere-
ly as types against which the male reactions can be measured."
For all his mysticism, Lawrence was singularly unperceptive
of women's needs and wants. He and the film are also discussed in a socio-political context.

*52   BLEVINS, WINIFRED. "Lawrence's Women in Love: Word to Image."
Los Angeles Herald Examiner (12 April), Section G, p. 4.
       [Cited in Zambrano, No. 350.]

1970

53   BURNE, JEROME. "The Music Lovers." Friends [London], No. 18
      (13 November), p. 20.
            Russell doesn't quite overcome the contrast between the
      dark of Tchaikovsky's life and the light expressed in his
      music; his biggest moments are the lurid incidents.

54   CANBY, VINCENT. "Lawrence's Philosophy in Subordinate Role."
      New York Times (26 March), p. 58.
            Women in Love sensuously captures "feeling of nature
      and of physical contact between people, and between people
      and nature." It also succeeds in making the Lawrentian
      point that the male-male relationships, though unfulfilled,
      are "less messy" than the male-female ones.

55   _____. Review of Women in Love. New York Times (29 March),
      Section 2, p. 1.
            Elaborates slightly on No. 54.

56   CARROLL, KATHLEEN. "Women in Love is Stunning Film." New
      York Daily News (26 March), p. 79.
            Review.

57   CRIST, JUDITH. "Love is a Many-Splendored Thing." New York,
      3 (30 March), 54-55.
            Women in Love is deeply beautiful and perfectly suited
      to the novel. Lawrence was precocious in his causes:
      emancipation of women, sexual freedom, spontaneity; the
      film is timely and could be exploitative, but is not.
      Kramer's screenplay is "brilliant," the sense of period
      striking, the cast fine. Russell manages to express vis-
      ually the passions, dualities, and sense of doom of the
      novel.

58   DE MAIO, DON. "Women in Love." Distant Drummer [Philadelphia],
      No. 82 (23 April), p. 9.
            Unlike most literary adaptations, this film captures
      the essence of its source.

59   DEMIDJUK, STANISLAV [and Ken Russell]. "The Films I Do Best
      Are About People I Believe In." Friends [London], No. 7
      (29 May), pp. 18-19.
            Russell discusses his ability to make expensive-looking
      films on a shoestring; his own films; and other people's
      films.

60   FRANCIS, MILLER, JR. "Women in Love." Great Speckled Bird
      [Atlanta], 3 (25 May), 21.
            Short review from the perspective of relevance, social
      change and female awareness.

61   GEDULD, HARRY M. "Lawrence, Sex and Celluloid." <u>Humanist</u>,
        30 (March/April), 31.
        <u>Women in Love</u> conveys "comparatively little of Lawrence's
        sexual credo" but has merits. Re-perusal of the book, af-
        ter seeing the film, emphasizes how far behind cinema is in
        developing ways of portraying sexual relationships. Con-
        temporary screen sex is discussed in relation to Lawrence's
        philosophy.

62   GERARD, LILLIAN N. "Of Lawrence and Love." <u>Film Library Quar-
        terly</u>, 3 (Fall), 6-12.
        <u>Women in Love</u> is faithful to the novel; Lawrence's
        philosophy is still timely, because his characters' ques-
        tionings, stirrings, needs and relationships are like those
        of people today. The film's main flaw is its need to <u>be</u>
        filmic.

63   GIBSON, JEREMY. "<u>Women in Love</u>." <u>Octopus</u> [Ottawa], 3 (19
        June), 15.
        Film captures novel's themes "without suffocating them,"
        although occasionally sidetracking to do one of Russell's
        "crowded set-pieces," or becoming "gimmicky." The film
        is weak on character, and curiously lacking in passion.

64   GOW, GORDON. "<u>Women in Love</u>." <u>Films and Filming</u>, 16 (Janu-
        ary), 49-50.
        Russell's images are "potent," the erotic scenes are
        "choreographed beautifully." The surprising amount of
        humor is "welcome," and the spiritual agony of the charac-
        ters is memorably portrayed. Flaws include choppiness
        and the exaggeration of the Hermione character.

65   _____ [and Ken Russell]. "Shock Treatment." <u>Films and Film-
        ing</u>, 16 (July), 8-12.
        Pre-release article on <u>The Music Lovers</u> quotes Russell
        extensively on his approach to the subject. He also brief-
        ly discusses his previous films. A paragraph of background
        information about the forthcoming <u>The Devils</u> is followed
        by a partial filmography.

66   HAMILTON, JACK and DAN McCOY. "<u>Women in Love</u>." <u>Look</u>, 34
        (24 February), 32-37.
        Photo article and text which points out Lawrence's and
        the film's major theme of the need for freedom to fully
        explore one's sexuality.

67   JACOBSON, DENISE. "<u>Women in Love</u>." <u>Willamette Bridge</u> [Port-
        land, Oregon], 3 (29 May), 22.
        The situations in the film are "hard to relate to the
        experience of today," but it "speaks eloquently on one
        level."

1970

68   KAEL, PAULINE. "Lust for 'Art.'" <u>New Yorker</u>, 46 (28 March),
      97-101.
           Russell has betrayed <u>Women in Love</u> by substituting big
      "purple" scenes for Lawrence's subtleties. He is "wildly
      imprecise," more concerned with style than clarity. The
      novel is used as a starting point, with "great assurance"
      but limited success. The characters, and the performances
      of the actors, are incomplete. The erotic sequences are
      too graphic in that the cinema hasn't developed conventions
      to successfully deal with such realism, and Russell even
      undercuts them by adding some existing screen symbolism to
      tell us "how it [the intercourse] was."

69   KAUFFMANN, STANLEY. Review of <u>Women in Love</u>. <u>New Republic</u>,
      162 (18 April), 20.
           The film isn't a successful adaptation of Lawrence.
      The proportions of talk to action are wrong, as are the
      emphases on certain incidents to the exclusion of others.
      The film is sometimes "too lush" and strives too much for
      effect in some spots--although others are handled quite
      nicely. Bates is wrong for Birkin but others are fine.

70   KNIGHT, ARTHUR. "Liberated Classics." <u>Saturday Review</u>, 53
      (21 March), 50-51.
           Brief discussion of former Lawrence films leads to men-
      tion of the innovations in <u>Women in Love</u>, and how they help
      express Lawrence's sexual philosophy. Russell understands
      the characters and what they were meant to represent; his
      sense of period is impressive; his visuals capture "the
      sensual immediacy of Lawrence's prose style."

71   KUHN, HELEN WELDON. "<u>Women in Love</u>." <u>Films in Review</u>, 21
      (April), 241-43.
           The novel is merely "a literary curiosity," and the
      film is "confusing," a "put-on" conceived for the purpose
      of displaying the private parts of its male cast.

72   LERMAN, LEO. "Love." <u>Mademoiselle</u>, 71 (May), 120.
           Russell succeeds beautifully in transferring <u>Women in
      Love</u> to the screen. He does well with passion and ideas
      and how they affect the characters. The actors are "mag-
      nificent."

73   MORGENSTERN, JOSEPH. "Body and Soul." <u>Newsweek</u>, 75 (6 April),
      97.
           In the film of <u>Women in Love</u>, the "relationships aren't
      there," leaving it a "series of sumptuously illustrated
      attitudes" with a good cast.

74 OGAR, RICHARD. "Women in Love Love." Berkeley Barb, 10 (1
    May), 17.
        Film "tends to emphasize plot and character...at the
    expense of Lawrence's philosophy and sexual mysticism,"
    but captures his mood.

75 OSTER, ART. "'I Want to Drown in Flesh....'" Kaleidoscope
    [Milwaukee], 3 (26 June), 10.
        Lawrence sometimes became too buried in symbolism; film,
    by its own symbolic nature, compounds the problem. Russell
    nearly makes Women in Love work, however; there are several
    "great" moments that never quite "merge into perfection."

76 PHILLIPS, GENE D. [and Ken Russell]. "An Interview with Ken
    Russell." Film Comment, 6 (Fall), 10-17.
        Russell discusses Women in Love, The Music Lovers and
    some of his TV films, particularly The Dance of the Seven
    Veils. Some of his directorial methods are: working fast
    (for spontaneity); improvisation on the set; and only work-
    ing with performers and crew who can intuit his needs.

77 REED, REX. Review of Women in Love. Holiday, 47 (June),
    21-22.
        Russell, "full of flash and poetry," gives good im-
    pressions of the Victorian atmosphere, but is ineffective
    with motivations and characters; he sacrifices clarity for
    style's sake.

78 REID, PHILLIPA. "Kensington Gore Comes to Cumberland." Lis-
    tener, 83 (19 February), 248-49.
        Humorous account of difficulties encountered by extras
    in The Dance of the Seven Veils.

79 RICE, SUSAN. Review of Women in Love. Media and Methods, 6
    (May), 12, 14.
        The film is talky without always being clear, and the
    ideas don't always work when they are made concrete. How-
    ever, Russell "composes with inspiration," and is "one of
    the poets of the medium."

80 RIPP, JUDITH. "Women in Love." Parents' Magazine, 45 (March),
    25.
        Notice calls film "powerful, thought-provoking," timely
    and tasteful.

81 ROTMAN, MEL. "Women in Love." Chevron [Waterloo, Canada], 11
    (13 November), 9.
        Review briefly discusses the kinds of love portrayed in
    the film, and remarks on the way it reveals women as "a
    potent and deadly force."

1970

82   SCHICKEL, RICHARD. "A Past Master in the Hands of a Future
One." Life, 68 (6 March), 14.
Women in Love is flawed, but Russell is "one of the most
exciting talents to appear in some time." Film has to bear
the brunt of Lawrence's "philosophical wrangles" in order
to do honor to the original work, which is itself flawed.
Part of the film's force comes from its method of gathering
and springing emotionally. It has a deep sense of period.

83   SCHLESINGER, ARTHUR, JR. "Women in Love: Fascinating Try."
Vogue, 155 (1 March), 114.
To those who know the novel, the film is "inadequate";
for those who don't it may be "incomprehensible." Russell,
unlike Lawrence, does not create the impression that the
mysteries left at the end have a solution.

84   SCHMITTROTH, JOHN, JR. "Bloody Mama vs. Blood Consciousness."
Metro [Detroit], 3 (7 May), 7.
Russell's direction of Women in Love is "sure and sensitive," the film is "a frightening and dreadful picture of
people unable to love."

85   SIEGEL, JOEL E. "Cinemagoing in London." DC Gazette, 1 (7
September), 12.
Women in Love is an indication of signs of life in
British cinema, despite its faults. These include a lack
of sensibility on Russell's part which makes him blow
things up into set-pieces, and his inability to handle
actors well.

86   SIMON, JOHN. "Lawrence In Print and On Film." New Leader,
53 (13 April), 26-28.
Lengthy essay on the novel Women in Love, followed by an
equally lengthy film review which enlarges on the initial
statement that the film is a "profound betrayal" of the
book.

87   SIRKIN, ELLIOTT. "Women in Love." Film Quarterly, 24 (Fall),
43-47.
Discusses the deficiencies of most film adaptations.
Women in Love is like a Masterplots précis. The characters
philosophize but do nothing. Too much time is spent on
dance scenes, on pretty visuals, and on unnecessary vig-
nettes which do not advance the plot. The cast is not
effective as an ensemble, the film is "seriously misguided"
and even the visual style is "affected."

88   _____. "Women in Love." Harry [Baltimore], 1 (1 June),
16-17.
Early version of No. 87.

89   STEWART, BRUCE. "Where There's Muck There's Polytheism."
     Month, 1 (February), 117-19.
          Both the novel and the film of Women in Love are rather
     pagan. The film is better than the book, since it pre-
     serves the integrity of Lawrence's thought and translates
     it into images. The film is like a quartet, having less a
     plot than a blend of themes.

90   SWEENEY, LOUISE. "Lawrence's Women Novel as a Film." Chris-
     tian Science Monitor [Eastern edition], 62 (April), 4.
          Women in Love is "so erotic...that it sensationalizes"
     Lawrence as it illustrates him. It is a rather dated per-
     iod piece, but a beautiful one with a "superb" cast. A
     few of the more self-indulgent and erotic sequences need
     cutting.

91   TARRATT, MARGARET. "An Obscene Undertaking." Films and Film-
     ing, 17 (November), 26-30.
          Long piece on Lawrence films--The Rocking-Horse Winner,
     Sons and Lovers, Lady Chatterly's Lover, The Fox and Women
     in Love. All have reflected the filmic style and ideology
     of the period in which they were made, but seldom have they
     really captured Lawrence; Women in Love comes closest so
     far. It is inadequate in its portrayal of the Ursula-
     Birkin relationship, but it doesn't try to avoid the im-
     plications of Lawrence's vision of the destructiveness of
     man-woman relationships. Crich's suicide illustrates part
     of the problem of filming Lawrence--the impossibility of
     pinning down the many levels of Lawrence's symbolism and
     the unwillingness of filmmakers to present Lawrence's
     "unpalatable" perceptions.

92   TUCKER, MARTIN. "Lawrence's Women." Commonweal, 92 (15 May),
     223.
          Précis of Lawrence's philosophy; review of Women in Love
     which doubts that it is really Lawrentian but praises its
     visual virtuosity. The "extremely sensuous tableaux" "stun
     the viewer with excitement" although much of the film fol-
     lows Lawrence's text but not his context.

93   WALSH, MOIRA. "Women in Love." America, 122 (25 April), 456.
          Film, like the film of Joyce's Ulysses, seems to be bits
     and pieces, just enough to convince the audience that it is
     seeing Lawrence. It is hard to tell whether flaws are due
     to weaknesses in the film itself or in Lawrence's philosophy.

*94   WARGA, WAYNE. "Kramer Scripts Thinking Man's Women in Love."
     Los Angeles Times Calendar (3 May), p. 12.
          [Cited in Zambrano, No. 350.]

1970

95 WEIGHTMAN, JOHN. "Trifling with the Dead." Encounter, 34
    (January), 50-53.
        Women in Love is good but should be better; there are
    unnecessary distortions and commercializations which, al-
    though they will probably increase the book's readership,
    will muddle the meaning. The book deals with class re-
    lationships and personal relationships, not entirely real-
    istically, particularly in the intermingling of classes.
    Some of the film's best scenes (although not the most Lawren-
    tian ones) are those in which Gudrun dances in front of the
    cattle, Crich subjugates his horse, and Birkin discusses
    figs. The erotic passages are sometimes boring (as in the
    most conventional couplings), sometimes good (the ambiguous
    nude scuffle), and sometimes puzzling.

96 WEINER, BERNARD. "Women in Love." Northwest Passage [Belling-
    ham, Washington], 3 (22 June), 22.
        Notice calls film "far inferior" to novel, offering
    only bits of Lawrence. It is an "oblique exercise which
    only fuzzes...up" the themes of the book.

97 WHITEHORN, ETHEL. "Women in Love." PTA Magazine, 64 (May),
    39.
        Notice says film is a "strong, beautiful" evocation of
    Lawrence.

                            1971

98 ALPERT, HOLLIS. "Sex Life of a Composer." Saturday Review,
    54 (30 January), 36.
        The Music Lovers' emphasis on the more "garish" events
    in Tchaikovsky's life leaves the impression that genius
    depends on an unfortunate sex life. Film is best when
    portraying Peter's relationship with Mme. von Meck.

99 ANON. "The Boy Friend." Filmfacts, 14: 469-73.
        Credits, synopsis, excerpts from popular press reviews.

100 ANON. "The Boy Friend." Time, 98 (20 December), 82-83.
        Photo preview.

101 ANON. "The Devils." Filmfacts, 14: 338-41.
        Credits, synopsis, excerpts from popular press reviews.

102 ANON. "The Devils." Good Times [San Francisco], 4 (15 Octo-
    ber), 24.
        Review.

103 ANON. "Director in a Caftan." Time, 98 (13 September), 53.
        Personality piece, written during the filming of The Boy
    Friend, stressing Russell's flamboyance.

104 ANON. "Ken Russell Films The Boy Friend." Films and Filming,
       18 (October), 34-35.
          Short article with background on the film and several
       production stills.

105 ANON. "Ken Russell's The Devils." Films and Filming, 17
       (July), 45-48.
          Photo preview.

106 ANON. "The Music Lovers." Filmfacts, 14: 146-49.
          Credits, synopsis, excerpts from popular press reviews.

107 ANON. "Music Lovers." Nola Express [New Orleans], No. 83
       (18 June), p. 21.
          Film seems biased in favor of homosexuality--women are
       all grotesque, men are all beautiful, etc.

108 ANON. Review of The Music Lovers. Playboy, 18 (April), 30.
          Russell is on a "cinematic binge" compared to his treat-
       ment of Women in Love. This is a film to forget.

109 ANON. "Segen fürs Kino." Der Spiegel, 25 (27 September),
       179-81.
          Review of The Devils and profile of Russell. In German.

110 ARNOLD, GARY. "The Devils at Dupont." Washington Post (13
       August), Section B, p. 11.
          Review.

111 _____. "Music Lovers." Washington Post (25 February),
       Section C, p. 14.
          Review.

112 AUSTIN, CHARLES M. "Religious Cinema at Its Best--and Worst."
       Christian Century, 88 (3 November), 1299-1300.
          The first part of the review--and the title--refers to
       Jacques Rivette's The Nun; the second, to The Devils, which
       is "swallowed by its own excesses." The horrors are so
       unrelenting that the audience has no time to think, or
       care, about the characters.

113 BAZAROV, KONSTANTIN. "The Music Lovers." [BFI] Monthly Film
       Bulletin, 38 (March), 53-54.
          Credits, synopsis, review which calls film "a crude
       melodrama about sex," particularly Tchaikovsky's homo-
       sexuality.

114 BILLINGTON, MICHAEL. "Ken Russell's Tchaikovsky." Illustrated
       London News, 258 (6 March), 32.
          In The Music Lovers, Russell's attempt at new forms of
       biography is laudable, but his own conventions are some-

1971

times ripe for parody. Tchaikovsky's and Russell's ex-
cesses are well-matched. "The success of the film hinges
on the intensity with which Russell communicates his personal vision of Tchaikovsky."

*115 BLUME, MARY. "Director Russell with Boy Friend: Ogre in a
Nursery?" Los Angeles Times Calendar (19 September), p. 18.
[Cited in Zambrano, No. 350.]

116 BRADFORD, T. I. "The Devils." It [London], No. 110 (12 August), p. 21.
Film's only purpose seems to be to let Russell indulge
himself.

117 BRUDNOY, DAVID. "Erotogenesis of Religion." National Review,
23 (5 November), 1250.
The Devils is "almost unbearably sadistic" and "stunning"
at the same time. Ultimately it is too much; a "smaller
scale" was needed for the story, not this "frenzied Holly-
wooden-headed extravaganza."

118 CANBY, VINCENT. "The Devils." New York Times (17 July),
p. 14.
Film is full of "clanking, silly, melodramatic effects,"
and is "less interested in coherent thought than in specta-
cle." This diminishes the meaning of the lives it portrays.

119 _____. "The Music Lovers." New York Times (25 January), p. 20.
The film goes to fantastic lengths, to "little ultimate
effect." The "nonstop hysteria" of the production over-
powers even the sensational plot. The Music Lovers is no
better in its way than the Hollywood biofictions: Russell
tells us more about himself as filmmaker than about Tchaikovsky.

120 CARE, ROSS. Review of The Devils. Lancaster Independent
Press, 3 (23 September), 7.
The film is deeply disturbing; despite its bad press,
it has relevance as an allegory above and beyond its bru-
tality. Occasional anachronisms mar its purity, as does
the lack of motivation on the part of the exorcist Barré;
still, it should be seen. Revised: No. 330.

121 CHAMPLIN, CHARLES. "The Games Devils Plays." Los Angeles
Times (16 July), Section 4, p. 1.
Review.

122 COCKS, JAY. "Madhouse Notes." Time, 98 (26 July), 50.
The Devils' "style and subject are perfectly matched"
to this "frighteningly effective" "glimpse of hell." The

"dewy" scenes between Grandier and his wife are less
effective as counterbalances to the insanity.

123 COHEN, LARRY. "The Music Lovers." Show, 2 (April), 50.
     Like Zeffirelli, Russell places picture before structure.
He tries to say that a man's life and art are total reflec-
tions of each other.

124 COLEMAN, JOHN. "Artists and Lovers." New Statesman, 81 (26
     February), 281.
     In The Music Lovers, Russell atones for his "whimsicali-
ty" and "perversity" with "heart-stopping images." He con-
veys the essence of Tchaikovsky's relationships well, although occasionally his imagination flags.

125 CRIST, JUDITH. Review of The Devils. New York, 4 (26 July),
     51.
     Film is foul, "a grand fiesta for sadists and sexual
perverts to revel in."

126 ____. Review of The Music Lovers. New York, 4 (1 February),
     54-55.
     The visually beautiful film is "shockingly bad"; two
hours of angst becomes "ludicrous," particularly when in-
flated with dream sequences. It is "a swirl of cinematic
self-indulgence, intellectual insult and incoherence."

127 CURTISS, THOMAS QUINN. "Venice Fete Cancels Public Showing of
     The Devils." New York Times (29 August), p. 55.
     News story and short review which says the story is the
"stuff of fine tragedy," although melodrama is emphasized
in the film.

128 DAWSON, JAN. "Tchap." Listener, 85 (4 March), 284.
     In The Music Lovers Russell suggests that genius is a
by-product of neuroses with "consummate vulgarity." His
imagery "affects the digestion of the spectator without
ever touching his intelligence."

129 DE MAIO, DON. "Blood." Thursday's Drummer [Philadelphia],
     No. 152 (19 August), p. 13.
     The Devils is a "headless freak" without love, plot,
character, or humor.

130 DRIVER, SUE. "The Devils." Georgia Straight [Vancouver, Can-
     ada], 5 (15 October), 19.
     Between the sources and the film, characterization is
lost. The literal representation of Jeanne's fantasies
makes them laughable; the subtlety of the Whiting play
is entirely lacking.

1971

131   EARLE, ANITRA. "Tchaikovsky's Life in The Music Lovers."
       San Francisco Chronicle (13 March), p. 34.
           Review.

132   FARBER, STEPHEN. "The Devils Finds an Advocate." New York
       Times (15 August), Section 2, p. 1.
           The film is "ambitious," a prophetic warning against the
       effects of ignorance. Russell's images are psychologically
       powerful. He finds it necessary to confront the idea of
       death and decay; in The Devils, Grandier's sensuality is
       "a rage against" death. The film is flawed, but filled
       with energy, passion and imagination. It seems to use
       history as a starting point for an allegory that is rele-
       vant today; but if this is what was intended, Russell's
       loving portrayal of exclusively seventeenth century tor-
       tures is disturbing.

133   _____. "A Dream Blasted by Sexual Reality." New York Times
       (21 February), Section 2, p. 11.
           The Music Lovers is bigger than life, as befits its
       romantic subject. Russell's delvings into psychoanalysis
       are exhilarating insights rather than case histories. The
       Tchaikovsky-Nina relationship embodies Russell's "most ur-
       gent theme--the startling disparity between imagination and
       reality." Some of Russell's sex scenes are "subtle" yet
       erotic, others are "highly charged" to the point of primi-
       tive fantasy. His vision of sex as a shatteringly powerful
       force makes The Music Lovers more Lawrentian than Women in
       Love.

134   GELATT, ROLAND. Review of The Devils. Saturday Review, 54
       (31 July), 50.
           Where Huxley's book is "an elegant exercise in histori-
       cal interpretation," notable for scathing irony and moral
       fervor, the film is "a sickening display of depravity and
       cruelty," full of "frenzied hyperbole and tawdry exhibi-
       tionism."

135   GILLETT, JOHN. "The Music Lovers." Sight and Sound, 40
       (Spring), 108-109.
           Film is "cold, unfeeling," predictable. Russell has
       "an enjoyment in the sheer act of film-making" which others
       lack, but he uses all his tricks at once.

136   GILLIAM, CARY. "The Devils." Harry [Baltimore], 2 (12 Octo-
       ber), 12, 15.
           Film is "powerfully grotesque" and affecting. Its
       cruelty is justified by its presentation of a near-tragedy
       and evocation of pity, as well as by its portrayal of real
       events which undermine our smug sense of being "civilized."

137 GILLIATT, PENELOPE. Review of The Devils. New Yorker, 47
       (24 July), 58-61.
            Film is historically and intellectually weak, as well
       as often "barbarous and silly" in its choice of emphases.
       Redgrave's performance is remarkable.

138 GOODWIN, JOHN. "The Devils." Space City [Houston], 3 (28
       October), 23.
            Film is half-ridiculous, half-"atrocious." It is Rus-
       sell's second-worst, but only because it is shorter than
       The Music Lovers.

139 GOW, GORDON. "The Devils." Films and Filming, 17 (September),
       49.
            Film's horrific scenes are effective; those concerning
       exorcism and Grandier's immolation are particularly power-
       ful.

140 _____. "The Music Lovers." Films and Filming, 17 (March),
       47-48.
            Film is "remarkable"; even the too frequent shock scenes
       are valid to the portrayal of Tchaikovsky's neurotic sensi-
       bilities as well as being "brilliantly cinematic." There
       is too much of Nina, but her scenes are powerful. The
       music is provocatively and evocatively matched to the image.

141 _____. "The Music Lovers." In International Film Guide 1972.
       Edited by Peter Cowie. London: Tantivy Press; New York:
       A. S. Barnes and Company, p. 103.
            Film has "much charm"; the music, even out of context,
       is appropriate; however, there is an "excess of ugliness."

142 GREENSPUN, ROGER. "The Boy Friend." New York Times (17 De-
       cember), p. 29.
            The film is an "honorable transformation" of the play.
       The sets are elaborate but witty, and the cast is "charm-
       ing."

143 GUARINO, ANN. "Devils Is Anti-Religious." New York Daily
       News (17 July), p. 26.
            Review.

144 HAMILTON, BECKY. "The Devils." Great Speckled Bird [Atlanta],
       4 (15 November), 7.
            Notice calls film "disgusting, completely decadent."

145 HARMETZ, RICHARD S. "'A Film in the Spirit of Tchaikovsky.'"
       Los Angeles Free Press, 8 (5 March), 19.
            In The Music Lovers, Russell succeeds in portraying the
       essence of Tchaikovsky, as well as of the "music lovers"
       in his life--Mme. von Meck, Nina, etc.--who resemble modern-
       day "groupies."

1971

146   HART, HENRY. "The Devils." Films in Review, 22 (August/Sep-
         tember), 437-38.
           Film is too entangled with Russell's psyche to be under-
         stood in itself. He confuses rather than clarifies his
         sources, but he still produces "a definite, albeit an emo-
         tional and irrational, effect."

147   HINELINE, KEITH. "The Devils." Harry [Baltimore], 2 (12 Octo-
         ber), 12.
           Film is "Goebbels in drag." Its catalog of excesses
         is its one and only purpose.

148   HOUSTON, PENELOPE. "Nun's Tale." The Times [London] (23
         July), p. 16.
           The Devils has no lucidity of argument and no clear
         indication of the kind of men Grandier's persecutors are.
         "It's forgivable to go too far; it's unforgivable to arrive
         back only at destinations long since deserted." Reed does
         a "respectable job" in an otherwise characterless gallery
         of grotesques.

149   HUDSON, CHRISTOPHER. Review of The Devils. Spectator, 227
         (24 July), 145.
           Film is "all expressionism and nothing expressed." The
         Whiting play had things to say about the "duplicity" and
         manipulation practiced by the Catholic Church; Russell for-
         sakes this for shots of excited nuns. The "style complete-
         ly swamps the content"--there is no normality in sight.

150   _____. "Roll Over, Tchaikovsky." Spectator, 226 (6 March),
         325.
           The Music Lovers enhances, not distorts, Tchaikovsky's
         life. The "magnificent razzmatazz of the music" and the
         lush visuals are often perfectly matched.

151   HUXLEY, ALDOUS. The Devils of Loudun. New York: Perennial
         Library, 374 pp.
           This edition of one of Russell's sources, an exhaustive
         account of the occurrences at Loudun, contains photos from
         the film.

152   KAEL, PAULINE. "Genius." New Yorker, 46 (30 January), 76-79.
           The fantasies in The Music Lovers belong to Russell more
         than to his characters. His approach is deliberately un-
         savory, opportunistically seizing on the worst side of
         every character and using shock scenes only to shock (rather
         than to inform). He defeats himself when his film becomes
         self-parody.

*153 KAHAN, SAUL. "Ken Russell, a Director Who Respects Artists."
       Los Angeles Times Calendar (28 March), p. 18.
          [Cited in Zambrano, No. 350.]

154   KANFER, STEFAN. "False Notes." Time, 97 (8 February), 82-83.
          In The Music Lovers, Tchaikovsky's sex life is viewed
       with the same intolerance that marred his own lifetime.
       Neither men nor women are treated well, while the music is
       used heavy-handedly to reveal psychology.

155   KAUFFMANN, STANLEY. Review of The Devils. New Republic, 165
       (11 September), 26-27.
          Russell thinks that one must be hysterical to make a
       film about hysteria. This one is a "farrago of witless
       exhibitionism" in which Redgrave, and especially Reed,
       perform well.

156   KAUFMAN, DEANNA. "Russell and Trumbo: Shock for Shock's
       Sake?" Chevron [Waterloo, Canada], 12 (10 December), 13.
          Compares critical reaction to The Devils with that to
       Johnny Got His Gun after separate comment on each film.
       The Devils is "visually shocking," a "firmly stated case
       against the Church and man's absurd treatment of himself."

157   KNICKERBOCKER, PAINE. "The Devils--a Lurid British Film."
       San Francisco Chronicle (19 August), p. 48.
          Review.

158   KNOLL, ROBERT F. "Women in Love." Film Heritage, 6 (Summer),
       1-6.
          In an extensive comparison with the novel, the film is
       seen as "uneven," stressing the novel's weaknesses and
       undermining its strengths.

159   LANGLEY, LEE. "Ken Russell: A Director Who Demands the Right
       to Be Outrageous." Show, 2 (October), 34-38.
          Article emphasizes Russell's flamboyance and discusses
       The Devils, with photos from the film and quotes from Rus-
       sell.

*160 _____. "The Right to Be Outrageous." Daily Telegraph [Lon-
       don] color supplement (9 July), pp. 18+.
          Possibly variant of No. 159. [Cited in British Humani-
       ties Index 1971, p. 365.]

161   LERMAN, LEO. "'Russell Chooses Blood to be Redder Than Brown.'"
       Mademoiselle, 74 (November), 136-37, 189-93.
          Light personality piece and interview with Russell and
       others: his wife, Oliver Reed, Glenda Jackson.

1971

162 McGOWEN, MARY. "Devils is Surreal Portrait." Iconoclast
[Dallas], 2 (3 September), 20.
Film has "all the taste and restraint of a three-day
gang-bang." The constant horrors undermine the impact of
Grandier's torture and death. A very talented cast and
crew are "sold out" for the sake of "art" and grotesquerie.

163 MAHAN, MIKE. "The Devils." Door [San Diego], 3 (27 October),
26.
Film succeeds due to its emotional impact. Some of its
problems, such as the almost unbelievable modernity of
Grandier and the political situation, are swept aside by
Grandier's force of character and the epic tide of events.

164 _____. "The Music Lovers." Door [San Diego], 3 (7 July),
11.
Russell is best when excessive, as in this film, in
which "history becomes part of form rather than content."
The realistic portions of the film are very unevenly acted
and directed, while the fantasy sequences seem neglected.

165 MALLETT, RICHARD. Review of The Devils. Punch, 261 (28 July),
129.
Film hysterically exaggerates the already sensational
story until it provokes "more uneasy laughter than horror."

166 _____. Review of The Music Lovers. Punch, 260 (3 March),
316.
In normal moments the film is all right, but "big
dramatic scenes bring tremendous, hysterical, sledge-
hammer exaggeration."

167 MANCINI, DAVID. "The Devils." Los Angeles News Advocate, 2
(1 November), 15.
Film is stunning but much weakened by Russell's incon-
sistencies.

*168 MANVELL, ROGER. "You Can Go to The Devils." Humanist [Brit-
ish], 86 (November), 331-33.
[Cited in British Humanities Index 1971, p. 365.]

169 MILLAR, GAVIN. Notice of The Devils. Listener, 86 (29 July),
156-57.

170 MILLER, EDWIN. "Spiffy Musical Spoof." Seventeen, 30 (December), 90-91, 132-34.
Profile of, and interview with, Christopher Gable; a
shorter one with Russell, on the set of The Boy Friend.

171 MILNE, TOM. "The Devils." [BFI] Monthly Film Bulletin, 38
     (August), 161-62.
          Credits, synopsis, review which says Russell approaches
     his subject as a tabloid newspaper would, forsaking analysis
     of socio-political motivations for naked nuns and kinky sex.

172 NORRIS, DAPHNE. "The Music Lovers." Films in Review, 22
     (March), 174-75.
          Little of the film is "intrinsically true" to Tchai-
     kovsky, and there is "little adequate use" of his music.
     The performances are poor, the musical performance "pro-
     saic"; the film is somehow still entertaining.

173 PORTERFIELD, CHRISTOPHER. "Russell: Spoofing the Spoof."
     Time, 98 (20 December), 87-88.
          The Boy Friend is too much of a good thing, unlike The
     Music Lovers and The Devils, which were "too much of a bad
     thing." Followed by a short piece on Russell.

174 POWER, VIKKI. "British Imports." Thursday's Drummer [Phila-
     delphia], No. 127 (4 March), pp. 7, 10.
          The Music Lovers is part of a Romantic revival, but
     poorly done so that it becomes uneven and unpleasant. "It
     could have been a beautiful symphony instead of a disso-
     nant cacophony."

175 RABAN, JONATHAN. "Homicidal Farce." New Statesman, 82 (30
     July), 151.
          The Devils is tasteless, touching, hysterical--Russell's
     best film to date. He has removed the humanism from his
     sources and restored the period's "sensualism" and "cruel-
     ty." "Reality turns into joke, and joke into nightmare."
     The two leads effortlessly shift back and forth between
     "a painfully eloquent, underplayed realism" and "libidinous
     cartooning."

176 REED, REX. "The Chords that Bind Are a Mix of Music, Hair-
     Raising Madness." New York Daily News (29 January), p. 56.
     Review of The Music Lovers.

177 _____. "Glenda Jackson and the Artistry of Insanity." New
     York Sunday News (24 January), p. 59.
          Jackson's work with Russell is one of the topics dis-
     cussed.

178 REYS, MICHAEL. Review of The Devils. Actuelle, No. 14
     (November), p. 29.
          In French.

1971

179   RICE, SUSAN. "Estival Festival." Media and Methods, 8 (Sep-
      tember), 8.
         The Devils is a mixture of "revolting excess" and
      genius--"poetic vision and incremental conceits that are
      as dazzling as they are inspired." At the same time, Rus-
      sell's style overwhelms the subject; it is a hard film to
      watch.

180   ____. "The Music Lovers." Take One, 2 (March), 29, 32.
         Film is a further development of the style that began to
      emerge in Russell's first films. He provides "richly
      sensuous surfaces" that the audience responds to directly.
      An account of the author's botched interview with Richard
      Chamberlain follows.

181   ____. "Trust Me--Go See The Music Lovers." Media and Meth-
      ods, 7 (March), 6, 10.
         Russell has in past films shown his knowledge of film
      history and his talent for capturing difficult ideas in
      images. In this film, his talent is distilled--good points
      kept, bad eliminated. Russell is a "mad poet" whose self-
      indulgence is just as viable as others' "elegant restraint."

182   RICK. "The Music Lovers." Variety, 261 (27 January), 17.
         Film is often grotesque, caring more for shock effects
      than it does for its subject.

183   RIPP, JUDITH. "The Devils." Parents' Magazine, 46 (Septem-
      ber), 12.
         Notice calls film "harrowing," with Reed dominating it.
      Russell builds it to an emotional crescendo, then somehow
      manages to take it higher for the finale.

184   ____. "The Music Lovers." Parents' Magazine, 46 (March),
      22.
         Notice says Russell's methods result in both "high-in-
      tensity" and "ridiculous" scenes.

185   ROBERTSHAW, URSULA. "Tchaikovsky on Film." Illustrated Lon-
      don News, 258 (9 January), 23.
         Pre-release article; background on Tchaikovsky and on
      The Music Lovers.

*186 ROSE, TONY. "Other People's Pictures." Movie Maker (May),
      pp. 300-303.
         Review of The Music Lovers. [Cited in Gomez, No. 578,
      p. 219.]

*187 ____. "Other People's Pictures." Movie Maker (October),
      pp. 650-52.
         Discusses Lourdes and The Devils. [Cited in Gomez, No.
      578, p. 219.]

188 SCHICKEL, RICHARD. "Great Lives on TV." Harper's, 242 (January), 28-33.
In his biopics, Russell has developed ways to portray
the act of creation and the moment of inspiration in ways
Hollywood could not. He refuses to hero-worship the Artist,
who seems, in his eyes, to be undermining, through egotisti-
cal ruthlessness in doing his work, the humane values that
should be upheld. Song of Summer is a case in point, as
are Dante's Inferno, Isadora Duncan and others.

189 _____. "Horror Show in a Convent." Life, 71 (24 September),
12.
Compared to the earlier films, which contained both
ugliness and beauty, The Devils is "nothing but disgust."
There is no human decency to be found in it; Russell has
wasted his "rare gift" on this film.

190 _____. "Tchaikovsky Unromanticized." Life, 70 (5 February),
12-13.
The Music Lovers provides strong contrasts: between
beauty and ugliness; between what we expect and what we
get. In his "big" moments, Russell is "drunk on the power
of film, on his own masterful and manic command of the
medium." He challenges the idea that creators of fine art
are fine people courageously and recklessly; with this
film, "he emerges as one of the great directors of our
era."

191 SCHLESINGER, ARTHUR, JR. "The Devils." Vogue, 158 (15
September), 88-89.
The story, combined with the style of "the Cecil B.
DeMille of the Freudian age" results in "overkill." The
film is gorgeous to look at, but the experience soon stops
being shattering and becomes "perverse."

192 SIEGEL, JOEL. "The Devils." D.C. Gazette, 2 (September), 14.
Short notice calls film "repulsive, perverted, certi-
fiably insane."

193 SINGER, HONEST BOB. "The Music Lovers." East Village Other
[New York], 6 (2 February), 19, 23.
Tchaikovsky "lends himself easily" to films. Russell's
version of him is interesting, although many of the performances are mediocre.

194 STEELE, LLOYD. "Grisly, Gutsy Masterpiece." Los Angeles Free
Press, 8 (23 July), 20.
A great many of Russell's own hang-ups are in The Devils,
but it is nonetheless breathtaking. It proves that Russell
is one of the "most controlled and...the least profound"

1971

filmic geniuses. The distortions of time, space, incident
may be the only way to give the seventeenth-century milieu
to audiences, but they also compromise the film, and characters are lost or stripped of the qualities that make
them sympathetic and believable. Still Russell has a
uniquely exciting way with his camera and the ability to
involve the audience emotionally.

195   STEWART, BRUCE. "Contrapunto Alla Mente: The Music Lovers."
      Month, 3 (May), 153.
         Russell uses the same tricks as Hollywood does, but the
      film still succeeds. The unconventional matchings of
      visuals and music are valid, the straying from historical
      fact annoying, the acting melodramatic; however, the film
      has a "curious and unforced beauty; that essential and
      always discernible quality which can make even a bad Ken
      Russell film better than many other people's good ones."
      This comes from an indefinable quality in Russell himself,
      in essence the ability to "see the skull beneath the skin."

196   _____. "Russell's Devils." Month, 4 (October), 122.
         The Devils is violent, vulgar, wilful and hysterical, and
      seems purposeless, unless Russell had a subconscious de-
      sire to make a film about one sane man in a mad world--an
      attractive theme for "a slightly critic-ridden movie man."
      He may have wanted to film a tragedy, but the film doesn't
      allow the audience to feel enough for the characters to
      make the tragedy work.

197   SWEENEY, LOUISE. "Movies--Twiggy, De Sica." Christian Sci-
      ence Monitor [Eastern edition], 64 (17 December), 4.
         The Boy Friend is "a movie musical that really works."
      Russell's unique style is evident; sometimes too much Bus-
      by Berkeley style decor is hurled at the audience. The
      cast is generally fine, and Tony Walton's design and Shir-
      ley Russell's costumes are outstanding.

198   _____. "Russell Films Devils Case." Christian Science Moni-
      tor [Eastern edition], 63 (17 July), 5.
         Notice calls film a "fetid exercise in sadism, debauch-
      ery, and profanity" as well as an "offensive mockery of
      Christianity."

199   _____. "Tchaikovsky Fiction." Christian Science Monitor
      [Eastern edition], 63 (17 February), 4.
         The images in The Music Lovers are beautiful, but
      blighted by the irony and ugliness of Russell's theme.

200   TAYLOR, JOHN RUSSELL. "Russell's Pathetic Fallacy." The
      Times [London] (24 February), p. 10.

Russell's talent is in evidence in The Music Lovers,
but it is misapplied. The film is too unrelentingly
hysterical, and Russell relies too much on the idea of
art reflecting life.

*201 TESSIER, MAX [and Ken Russell]. "Entretien avec Ken Russell"
      [Interview with Ken Russell]. Cinéma (December), p. 119.
      [Cited in Gomez, No. 578, p. 223.]

*202 ____. "The Music Lovers: La Vie Privée Sexuelle de Piotr
      Illytch" [The Private Sexual Life of Piotr Illytch].
      Cinéma (March), pp. 131-34.
      [Cited in Gomez, No. 578, p. 223.]

203   THOMAS, KEVIN. "Life of Troubled Composer." Los Angeles
      Times (24 February), Section 4, pp. 1, 11.
      Review of The Music Lovers.

204   VERR. "The Devils." Variety, 263 (14 July), 16.
      Russell's "frenzied" approach sends film "over the
      brink," emphasizing the gruesome at the expense of dramatic
      coherence.

205   WALSH, MOIRA. "Communication Vs. Challenge." America, 125
      (4 September), 126-27.
      Russell loses The Devils' story amid "sound and fury."
      The needed "sign of the human spirit at work," embodied
      for both Huxley and Whiting in Grandier, is overwhelmed
      by the grotesque.

206   ____. "The Music Lovers." America, 124 (27 February), 209.
      Film is "hyperthyroid." Russell, with his "enormous
      but undisciplined flair for evocative cinematic images"
      almost makes the overblown scenes work, and his recreation
      of the period is superior.

207   WEIGHTMAN, JOHN. "How Not to Love Music." Encounter, 36
      (May), 48-50.
      Russell has prematurely reached "artistic absurdity."
      If The Music Lovers is meant to be taken seriously, it
      illustrates two "philistine principles that need damning."
      The adaptor has no right to tamper as he pleases with his
      sources, to present truth, half-truth, and lies without
      distinguishing amongst them. And art is not a direct re-
      flection of the artist's life, but rather a "transmuta-
      tion" of experience. Russell imposes arbitrary imagery on
      the music, which should be "its own truth."

208   WESTERBECK, COLIN L., JR. "The Nun's Story." Commonweal, 95
      (1 October), 16-17.

> In The Devils, the shift of the Loudun walls controversy from peripheral to central importance in Grandier's life distorts him into a political, and thus modern, hero. Russell's willingness to abandon history, narrative, and character in favor of a portrayal of "corruption in man and nature" amounts to a kind of pornography.

209 WHIT. "The Boy Friend." Variety, 265 (22 December), 6.
    Film is "novel, engaging," although editing sometimes "misses its point."

210 WHITEHORN, ETHEL. "The Music Lovers." PTA Magazine, 65 (March), 39.
    Notice calls film "lurid," "depraved."

211 WILLIAMS, BRUCE. "The Devils." Nola Express [New Orleans], No. 92 (21 October), p. 18.
    Russell handles this large-scale film "superbly," and in Grandier creates a true hero.

212 ZACHARY, RALPH. "Three Composers." Opera News, 35 (27 February), 33.
    The Music Lovers is "third-rate melodrama" which seems to use its subject as an excuse for an exercise in lush camera effects. It fails to illuminate Tchaikovsky's life.

213 ZIMMERMAN, PAUL D. "Back to Never-Never Land." Newsweek, 78 (27 December), 61-62.
    The Boy Friend is a "roaring, opulent" tribute to '30s musicals which is at once funny, dazzling and touching. The cast is fine; Twiggy is "perfect."

214 _____. "Over the Edge." Newsweek, 78 (26 July), 70-72.
    At times Russell's appetite for the bizarre has worked in his favor, but in The Devils he goes "beyond extravagance to insanity." The ugliness does not obscure the simplemindedness of the film, and possibly of its director.

215 _____. "Tonight We Love." Newsweek, 77 (8 February), 94.
    In The Music Lovers, Russell captures the spirit of Tchaikovsky's music, and uses the music effectively to convey emotion; however, the screenplay is cliché-ridden and shallow.

1972

216 AMBROSE, PAUL F. "'Twiggy,' I Cried, 'I Love You.'" Daily Planet [Miami], 1 (10 August), 27.
    Review of The Boy Friend.

*217   ANON. "Ken Russell and <u>Savage Messiah</u>." <u>After Dark</u> (21
       November), p. 38.
       [Cited in Gomez, No. 578, p. 221.]

218   ANON. Review of <u>The Boy Friend</u>. <u>Playboy</u>, 19 (March), 30.
       Twiggy is the film's major asset. Russell's parody of
       a parody somehow succeeds.

219   ANON. "<u>Savage Messiah</u>." <u>Filmfacts</u>, 15 (1972), 578-82.
       Credits, synopsis, excerpts from popular press reviews.

220   ARNOLD, GARY. "<u>The Boy Friend</u>." <u>Washington Post</u> (28 January),
       Section D, pp. 1, 11.
       The potential sweetness of the film is marred by Rus-
       sell's "self-serving" misuse of Twiggy and Tommy Tune, and
       the "wrongheadedness, the misconceptions, and the vulgarity"
       of his approach. This is emphasized by the production
       numbers which, unlike Berkeley's, have a blatant, rather
       than innocent, sexual slant.

221   AXELSSON, SUN. "Vårt Behov av Skräck" [What We Demand of
       Horror]. <u>Chaplin</u>, 14: 8-11.
       Compares <u>The Devils</u> with Arrabal's <u>Viva la Muerte</u>. In
       Danish.

222   BILLINGTON, MICHAEL. "Energy and Allegory." <u>Illustrated Lon-
       don News</u>, 260 (November), 79.
       In <u>Savage Messiah</u>, Russell is very good at conveying
       the idea that creation is "damned hard work," and at por-
       traying the Brzeska-Gaudier relationship. His flaw is his
       "facetious" view of the Vorticist movement.

223   _____. "Lively <u>Boy Friend</u>." <u>Illustrated London News</u>, 260
       (March), 58.
       Russell is an extraordinary talent, incapable of being
       dull; this film is flawed only by the lack of contrast
       between the stage production and the De Thrill version.

224   BRUDNOY, DAVID. Review of <u>The Boy Friend</u>. <u>National Review</u>,
       24 (28 April), 476.
       Notice says film "rarely rises above frantic tedium."

225   BUCKLEY, PETER [and Ken Russell]. "Savage Saviour." <u>Films
       and Filming</u>, 19 (October), 12-16.
       Russell discusses <u>Savage Messiah</u>; Buckley defines Rus-
       sell's recurring themes as "the artist at odds with society;
       creation versus subsistence; love and hate battling away in
       the soul of genius; flesh and the devil."

1972

226   CANBY, VINCENT. Review of Savage Messiah. New York Times (9
      November), p. 55.
          Film is incomplete; the audience is not told what
      Gaudier is "up to," why his art endures, what Sophie is
      thinking, etc.

227   CARE, ROSS. Review of The Boy Friend. Lancaster Independent
      Press, 4 (17 February), 8, 11.
          The film is an "innovative cinema masterpiece." Its
      adaptation of the intimate musical is inspired, the specta-
      cle is breathtaking, but there are also moments of "ex-
      quisite simplicity" which recall the "visual power" of
      some of Russell's earlier films.

228   CARTER, CURTIS L. "The Boy Friend." Bugle American [Milwau-
      kee], 3 (16 February), 21.
          The play is imaginatively adapted into a film full of
      "fanciful images."

229   CIGLIČ, M. "Demoni" [The Devils]. Ekran, 10-11: 100-101.
      Review. In Serbo-Croatian.

230   CIMENT, MICHEL. "Savage Messiah." Positif, No. 144-45 (No-
      vember/December), pp. 90-91.
          Review.

231   COLEMAN, JOHN. Review of The Boy Friend. New Statesman, 83
      (4 February), 154.
          "Russell has found the perfect objective correlative
      for his extravagant turn of image" in the three-story
      device. Twiggy is "exquisite."

232   _____. "Rich, Not Gaudier." New Statesman, 84 (15 September),
      368.
          There is an element of "self-portraiture" in Russell's
      Gaudier in Savage Messiah. He also seems to be trying to
      find a larger audience without too much compromise, but he
      cannot. Tutin's strong performance as Sophie Brzeska ul-
      timately harms the film by changing its focus to her.

233   COMBS, RICHARD. "Savage Messiah." [BFI] Monthly Film Bulle-
      tin, 39 (October), 217.
          Credits, synopsis, review which says that Russell
      creates a "spectacle" in which the "trumpeting of emotion
      is unrelated to any dramatic, or credibly human, concept
      of character"; it is "the illusion of an illusion, the
      vastly inflated advertisement for a drama."

234   COMUZIO, ERMANNO. "Il Boy Friend." <u>Cineforum</u>, No. 115-16,
      (July/August).
         Compares and contrasts the Russell film with the original
      Sandy Wilson play. In Italian.

235   CRIST, JUDITH. Review of <u>Savage Messiah</u>. <u>New York</u>, 5 (13
      November), 131.
         The character of Henri Gaudier is made real by that of
      Sophie Brzeska. The clichéd script and "near-camp" direc-
      tion allow "artifices" to take over and falsify the rest
      of the film.

236   _____. "Some Late Bloomers, and a Few Weeds." <u>New York</u>, 5
      (10 January), 57.
         In his treatment of <u>The Boy Friend</u>, Russell has bloated
      Wilson's "tiny gem" of a pastiche with "globs and globs
      of creamy campy over-production."

237   CUTLER, BILL. "<u>Savage Messiah</u>." <u>Great Speckled Bird</u>
      [Atlanta], 5 (4 December), 14.
         Review.

238   DAWSON, JAN. "<u>The Boy Friend</u>." <u>Sight and Sound</u>, 41 (Spring),
      111-12.
         In each film, Russell first trivializes his sources,
      then makes the result epic. He robs this film of its nos-
      talgia, overbalancing the "slight" songs with overdone pro-
      duction numbers. The only aspect of the film that works is
      Twiggy.

239   DELANEY, MARSHALL. Review of <u>The Boy Friend</u>. <u>Saturday Night</u>,
      87 (February), 43.
         Russell differs from Berkeley in that the latter knew
      when to stop.

240   DEMPSEY, MICHAEL. "The World of Ken Russell." <u>Film Quarter-
      ly</u>, 25 (Spring), 13-25.
         Discusses <u>The Music Lovers</u> and <u>The Devils</u>; Russell's
      mixture of skepticism and admiration in his treatment of
      "heroes"; his use of historical persons (artists) as pre-
      texts to study how they relate to art and life; his visual
      style; his continuing theme of "transcendence."

241   FISHER, JACK. "Three Paintings of Sex: the Films of Ken
      Russell." <u>Film Journal</u>, 2 (September), 32-43.
         Analyzes <u>Women in Love</u>, <u>The Music Lovers</u> and <u>The Devils</u>,
      visually (as kinetic paintings in different styles, whose
      moods and messages are conveyed through painterly use of
      color, line, form, etc.); and thematically (as essays on,
      respectively, sexual relationships, homosexuality, and devi-
      ant sex expressed primarily as religio-eroticism). Re-
      printed in No. 568.

1972

242　FLATLEY, GUY [and Ken Russell]. "'I'm Surprised My Films
　　　Shock People.'" New York Times (15 October), p. 15.
　　　　　Russell discusses his films past, present, and future;
　　　censorship; other directors' films.

243　FULLER, STEVEN. "The Boy Friend." Rolling Stone, No. 104
　　　(16 March), p. 66.
　　　　　Film is "original and inspired," a departure from Rus-
　　　sell's earlier films, with their themes of death, torture
　　　and homosexuality. He is emerging as one of the Seventies'
　　　most influential directors, although his body of work is
　　　still small.

244　GEDULD, HARRY M. "Going to the Devil." Humanist [U.S.], 32
　　　(January/February), 33-34.
　　　　　The Devils is "mainly concerned with revealing the con-
　　　sequences of allowing the Church (or any other religious
　　　organization) to wield political power." It is weakened
　　　by some of the secondary players and by its disregard for
　　　Sister Jeanne's problems.

245　GOW, GORDON. "Savage Messiah." Films and Filming, 19 (Octo-
　　　ber), 45.
　　　　　Film is unexpectedly tender as it quietly evokes the
　　　curious relationship of its protagonists.

246　GREEN, BENNY. Review of Savage Messiah. Punch, 263 (20 Sep-
　　　tember), 386-87.
　　　　　Russell has heretofore earned a footnote in history by
　　　"achieving...the apparently impossible feat" of making D.
　　　G. Rossetti boring, and by doing similar harm to musicians.
　　　Savage Messiah is different; it is "compassionate" and "mag-
　　　nificently acted," especially by Tutin.

247　GREEN, JONATHON. "The Boy Friend." It [London], No. 123 (10
　　　February), p. 20.
　　　　　Film is colorful and fun on a non-serious level, and
　　　Twiggy is surprisingly, though not profoundly, talented.

248　HARDAWAY, FRANCINE. "Crazy Ken Russell." New Times [Tempe,
　　　Arizona], 3 (15 March), 18.
　　　　　The Boy Friend has a leering, unwholesome quality in
　　　the frame story; the musical numbers are "amusing" and
　　　Twiggy performs well.

249　HAWK. "Savage Messiah." Variety, 268 (13 September), 24.
　　　　　There is "more style than warmth" in the relationships,
　　　with "deep-down feeling" only occurring near the end.
　　　Still, there is charm and "panache" in Russell's treatment.

250 HIRSCH, PETER. "Djaevlenes Falske Martyrglorie." Chaplin,
14: 65-66.
Review of The Devils. In Danish.

251 HOUSTON, PENELOPE. "The Boy Friend." [BFI] Monthly Film
Bulletin, 39 (March), 48.
Credits, synopsis, review which says that the film
rather uncertainly wavers between the three levels it
operates on. The Berkeleyish numbers lack the master's
touch.

252 HUDSON, CHRISTOPHER. "Puppets in Love." Spectator, 229 (16
September), 440.
Russell caricatures "everything he touches," including,
in Savage Messiah, Gaudier and Brzeska; it is sad, because
he could do better with his "prodigious gifts."

253 HUGHES, ROBERT. "Erratic Bust." Time, 100 (20 November), 98,
K18.
Gaudier and Brzeska are treated well, but the rest of
Savage Messiah is caricature.

254 KAEL, PAULINE. "Hyperbole and Narcissus." New Yorker, 48
(18 November), 225-32.
In this very complex review of Savage Messiah, Russell
is characterized as having "flair...imagination and...force"
but "little actual command" of film technique. This film
looks like a Hollywood product, with its distortions; the
parodies within it are also off-target. Russell's films
"not consciously...but instinctively" "cheapen everything
they touch."

255 _____. "Pleasing and Punishing." New Yorker, 47 (8 January),
24-27.
The play of The Boy Friend succeeded because it not
only parodied the old-style musicals, but also had a feeling of nostalgia for them. Russell has no feeling at all;
he turns the story into anti-show business satire. His
reduction of the story to a "revue" would still be tolerable
but for the lack of a "first-rate" performer other than
Tommy Tune; Russell fails to make Twiggy into anything but
a "blank."

256 KERMAUNER, T. "Želje in Hudiči." Ekran, 10: 313-19.
Thorough discussion of The Devils. In Serbo-Croatian.

257 KNIGHT, ARTHUR. Review of Savage Messiah. Saturday Review,
55 (25 November), 79.
Notice says that Savage Messiah poses much the same ques-
tion The Music Lovers did--where does Tchaikovsky leave off
and Russell begin?--without The Music Lovers' "breathtaking
imagery" to compensate.

1972

258   ____. "Won't You Charleston With Me?" <u>Saturday Review</u>, 55
       (29 January), 23.
            The studio's cutting of <u>The Boy Friend</u> hurts the "de-
       lightfully and delicately executed" film. The parodies of
       the old greats are "deft and elegant," knowing and affec-
       tionate. Twiggy, while not overly talented, has an endear-
       ing presence.

259   KOCH, DON. "<u>Savage Messiah</u>." <u>Straight Creek Journal</u> [Denver
       and Boulder], 1 (5 December), 11.
            Film is "coherent," well-paced; its parts are integrated;
       it employs no gimmicks, only fine acting photography, and
       editing; it is a "wholly satisfying film experience."

260   LA POLLA, FRANCO. "Riflessioni Sul Musical (a Proposito di Un
       Film 'Inglese' di Ken Russell)." <u>Filmcritica</u>, 13 (Novem-
       ber/December), 402-408.
            Discusses <u>The Boy Friend</u>, thoroughly and technically,
       from several perspectives. In Italian.

261   LATO, DENNIS. Review of <u>Savage Messiah</u>. <u>Express</u> [Hicksville,
       N.Y.], 1 (16 November), 17.
            Although lacking subtleties, Russell films are "passion-
       ate and opulent displays." <u>Savage Messiah</u> shows a loss of
       spontaneity and a lack of excitement.

262   LEAYMAN, CHARLES D. Review of <u>Savage Messiah</u>. <u>Lancaster Inde-
       pendent Press</u>, 4 (8 December), 7.
            Film is "brimming with movement...and an unexpectedness
       and sense of surprise." It is Russell's finest and most
       personal theatrical feature.

263   LEFÈVRE, RAYMOND. "<u>The Boy Friend</u>." <u>Cinéma</u>, No. 167 (June),
       p. 153.
            Film is entertaining, but quickly eclipsed by the origi-
       nals it mocks. For Russell it is a pleasant diversion.
       In French.

264   ____. "<u>The Boy Friend</u>." <u>Image et Son</u>, No. 262 (June/July),
       pp. 90-91.
            The film is a rest between Russell's cinematic "storms";
       his sense of the outrageous can be seen lurking in it. In
       French.

*265   LEROUX, A. "<u>The Boy Friend</u>." <u>Cinéma Que</u>, 1 (March/April),
       36-37.
            [Cited in <u>International Index to Film Periodicals 1972</u>,
       p. 128.]

266   LEVINE, JOAN. "<u>The Boy Friend</u>." <u>Door</u> [San Diego], 3 (30
       March), 23.

> Most Russell films have "gut-level" appeal. This one
> doesn't succeed as well because it tries to appeal to every-
> one. The musical sequences are exciting and colorful, the
> film worth seeing.

267   LEVINE, JOAN. Review of <u>Savage Messiah</u>. <u>Door</u> [San Diego], 4
      (20 December), 21.

268   LOCHTE, DICK. "Savage Messiah." <u>Los Angeles Free Press</u>, 9
      (20 October), Section 1, p. 10.
         Russell presents the film's relationships with rare
      qualities of "control, economy, and taste." He falters
      somewhat in the bits of broad comedy.

269   LOGUE, CHRISTOPHER. "<u>Savage Messiah</u>." <u>Films and Filming</u>, 19
      (November) 28-29.
         Screenplay excerpt.

270   LÖTHWALL, L.-O. "<u>Vildsint Messias</u>" [<u>Savage Messiah</u>]. <u>Chaplin</u>,
      14: 256-57.
         Review. In Swedish.

271   LUCATO, CLAUDIO, ed. "<u>Donne in Amore</u>." <u>Cineforum</u>, 12 (Jan-
      uary/February), 113-27.
         Discussion of some Lawrence films and very thorough
      analysis of <u>Women in Love</u>: plot synopsis, sections on
      misogyny in the film; "society, nature and death"; Russell's
      treatment of the material, and partial credits. In Italian.

272   LUNDBERG, CLAES. "<u>Boy Friend</u>." <u>Chaplin</u>, 14: 230-31.
         Review. In Swedish.

*273   MacDONOUGH, SCOTT [and Oliver Reed]. "Britain's Volatile
      Oliver Reed: 'I Only Bully Bigger Bullies!'" <u>Show</u> (April),
      pp. 32-37.
         Interview touches on Reed's work for Russell. [Cited
      in Gomez, No. 578, p. 222.]

274   McGOWEN, MARY. "<u>Boy Friend</u> Satirical Extravaganza." <u>Icono-
      clast</u> [Dallas], 6 (17 March), 12.
         Film is "strictly entertainment," pleasantly "silly and
      unabashedly nostalgic."

275   MALLETT, RICHARD. Review of <u>The Boy Friend</u>. Punch, 262 (9
      February), 193.
         The film is "an enjoyable success"; the feeling is nos-
      talgic, and Twiggy has definite star quality.

276   MANVELL, ROGER. "Russell, Ken." In <u>International Encyclopedia
      of Film</u>. Edited by Roger Manvell and Lewis Jacobs. New
      York: Crown Publishers, p. 424.

1972

>   List of Russell's films and quick analysis of his style;
> he has an affinity to von Sternberg or Ophüls without "their
> precise filmic judgement."

277   MASLIN, JANET. "Savage Messiah." Rolling Stone, No. 124 (21
      December), p. 72.
>   This is Russell's "most purely enjoyable" film. The
> scene in which Gaudier, drawing, ignores an anatomy book
> in favor of his own left hand--"the finished product bears
> little resemblance to the standard textbook version, but
> it has a fine, original beauty all its own"--resembles Rus-
> sell's own method.

278   MAURIAC, CLAUDE. "Ken Russell et le Sculpteur Français."
      L'Express, No. 1120 (25 December), p. 44.
>   Review of Savage Messiah. In French.

279   MILLAR, GAVIN. "Bezazz." Listener, 87 (10 February), 192-93.
>   At times, The Boy Friend goes beyond parodying old musi-
> cals to "recapture the brilliance of the originals." Twig-
> gy is irresistible.

280   MILLER, EDWIN. "The Boy Friend." Seventeen, 31 (February),
      96.
>   Notice calls film a "campy showpiece."

*281 MUŽIČ, N. "Zaljubljene Ženske" [Women in Love]. Ekran, 10:
      224.
>   Review. In Serbo-Croatian. [Cited in International
> Index to Film Periodicals 1972, p. 249.]

*282 O'BRIEN, GLENN. "Ken Russell in the Port of New York." Inter/
      View, 27 (November), 9-11.
>   [Cited in International Index to Film Periodicals 1972,
> p. 318.]

*283 _____. "Savage Messiah." Inter/View, 27 (November), 40-41.
>   [Cited in International Index to Film Periodicals 1972,
> p. 220.]

284   OLDENBURG, JORGEN. "Djaevlene (1)" [The Devils (1)]. Kosmo-
      rama, 18 (February), 136-37.
>   Review. In Danish. See No. 310.

285   PALMER, TONY. "D'Ye Ken Russell?" Spectator, 228 (5 February),
      205-206.
>   Russell does indulge in excess, but he is a visual
> virtuoso with a fresh approach to his subjects and a live-
> ly sense of self-parody.

286 PECHTER, WILLIAM S. "Movie Musicals." Commentary, 53 (May),
    77-78.
      Russell's adaptation of The Boy Friend is "loveless."
    He resembles De Thrill as he dreams of using the thin play
    he's watching to display his own virtuosity. The tedium of
    some of the Berkeley material Russell condescendingly paro-
    dies is well matched by that of the parodies themselves.

287 PÉREZ, MICHEL. "Un Exercice de Piété Hypocrite." Positif,
    No. 139 (June), pp. 51-54.
      Long analysis of The Boy Friend says that it, even more
    than The Devils, displays the "snobbism and opportunism"
    of Ken Russell.

288 POWELL, DILYS. "Guying the Dolls." Sunday Times [London] (6
    February), p. 28.
      Review of The Boy Friend.

289 _____. "The Sorcerer's Apprentice." Sunday Times [London] (17
    September), p. 36.
      Review of Savage Messiah.

290 REILLY, CHARLES PHILLIPS. "The Boy Friend." Films in Review,
    23 (January), 52-53.
      Film is "almost a work of art" with its "ingenious fan-
    tasy and satire," its solid cast, and its happy ending.

291 _____. "Savage Messiah." Films in Review, 23 (November),
    571.
      Russell displays both "brilliance" and "ineptitude" in
    this flawed film which nevertheless "moves."

292 RICE, SUSAN. Review of The Boy Friend. Media and Methods, 8
    (February), 15.
      After the excesses of the earlier films, this "innocu-
    ous" one is "attenuated and uninspired," the production
    numbers "loveless, lifeless."

293 _____. "Savage Messiah." Media and Methods, 9 (November), 12.
      Notice calls film a "loveless biography" without a glim-
    mer of Russell's personality.

294 RIPP, JUDITH. "Savage Messiah." Parents' Magazine, 47 (Novem-
    ber), 38.
      Notice.

295 RONAN, MARGARET. "RX for the Blahs and the Blues." Senior
    Scholastic, 100 (28 February), 23.
      Review of The Boy Friend.

1972

*296   ROSE, TONY. "On the Set with Ken Russell." Movie Maker (Sep-
           tember), pp. 618-19.
                [Cited in Gomez, No. 578, p. 223.]

*297   _____. "Other People's Pictures." Movie Maker (April), pp.
           244-47.
                Compares Russell with Kubrick. [Cited in Gomez, No.
           578, p. 219.]

 298   SCHEPELERN, PETER. "The Boy Friend." Kosmorama, 18 (Septem-
           ber), 273-74.
                Review. In Danish.

 299   SCHICKEL, RICHARD. "Savage Take-Off of a Put-On." Life, 72
           (21 January), 16.
                The Boy Friend is a "weird and maniacal...marvelously
           energizing" collation of every musical comedy cliché.
           Underneath the surface fun is the sub-story of the hope-
           lessly ambitious troupe which represents "human vanity
           and vacuity" at the "silliest, saddest level."

 300   SIEGEL, JOEL E. Review of The Boy Friend. D. C. Gazette, 3
           (9 February), 14.

 301   _____. Review of Savage Messiah. D. C. Gazette, 4 (8 Novem-
           ber), 13.

 302   SIMON, JOHN. Review of Savage Messiah. New Leader, 55 (11
           December), 30.
                Film is the usual Russell flight of fancy and fabrication,
           in which the artist becomes a "psychopath." Dorothy Tutin's
           performance "glows like a jewel inside a pig's bladder."

 303   _____. "Vulgarity With a Vengeance." New Leader, 55 (7 Feb-
           ruary), 22-23.
                The Boy Friend is well above the usual Russell fare; it
           gives the innocent play a cutting edge of satire by show-
           ing the backstage tawdriness of the provincial troupe, as
           well as investing it with a sort of kinkiness in the big
           Berkeleyish numbers. Twiggy successfully makes the trans-
           ition from model to actress, conveying an infectious inno-
           cence.

 304   SISKEL, GENE. "The Boy Friend." Chicago Tribune (7 February),
           Section 2, p. 15.
                Film is a "mostly entertaining, always dazzling trip
           through Campsville." Its major flaw is the confused edit-
           ing of the three stories; its major asset is Twiggy.

305 STERRITT, DAVID. "Portrait of the Artist in Russell Film."
     Christian Science Monitor [Eastern edition], 64 (2 Novem-
     ber), 4.
          Savage Messiah is charming when it is allowed to be;
     its main strength lies in the relationship of Henri and
     Sophie.

306 TAYLOR, JOHN RUSSELL. "The Artist as Exhibitionist." The
     Times [London] (15 September), p. 9.
          In Savage Messiah, as in previous films, Russell is bad
     but never boring. He fails to really explain Gaudier, mak-
     ing him loud and vulgar without illuminating his art. The
     film is "infuriating" because the talent that has gone into
     it is "perversely...turned against itself."

307 _____. "The Boy Friend." The Times [London] (1 February),
     p. 10.
          Review.

308 TERRY, CARROLL. "The Boy Friend." Good Housekeeping, 174
     (February), 66.
          Notice calls film "a spectacular, glittering, 'old-
     fashioned' family movie."

309 TESSIER, MAX. "The Boy Friend." Écran, 7 (July/August),
     72-73.
          Film is aesthetically pleasing, the parody is clever,
     the casting, especially of Twiggy, is fine. In French.

310 THOMSEN, CHR. BRAAD. "Djaevlene (2)" [The Devils (2)]. Kosmo-
     rama, 18 (February), 137-38.
          Review. In Danish. Companion piece to Oldenburg, No.
     284.

311 TROELLER, GORDIAN. "Savage Messiah." It [London], No. 138
     (18 September), p. 22.
          Film is like a symphony in which separate parts seem
     to clash, but merge at the end into a complete work. Rus-
     sell's finest film to date is "as harrowing as The Devils
     but on a subtler level."

312 TURRONI, GIUSEPPE. "Il Boy Friend." Filmcritica, 13 (April/
     May), 202-203.
          Compares The Boy Friend (and Russell's other films) with
     the work of several other directors. In Italian.

313 _____. "Donne in Amore" [Women in Love]. Filmcritica, 13
     (March), 153.
          Review. In Italian.

1972

*314 VACULÍKOVÁ, B. "10/bv." Film a Doba, 18 (January), 52.
      Review of The Devils. In Czech. [Cited in International
      Index to Film Periodicals 1972, p. 149.]

315   VIRGINIA. Notice of The Devils. Seed [Chicago], 8 (13 Janu-
      ary), 29.

316   WADE, VALERIE. "The Girl Friend." Sunday Times Magazine
      [London] (2 January), pp. 18-22.
      Interview with Shirley Russell, discussing her work as
      costume designer for The Boy Friend.

317   WARNER, ALAN. "The Boy Friend." Films and Filming, 18
      (April), 49-50.
      Russell has "an understanding of and a yearning for the
      cinema in its most flamboyant and visceral form." The Boy
      Friend's musical numbers are extraordinarily inventive, but
      Russell is in danger of overstepping his homage to Berkeley.
      Twiggy is unexpectedly perfect.

318   WEINSTEIN, ANITA. "The Boy Friend." Argo [Pomona, N. J.], 3
      (24 March), 23.
      Review.

319   WESTERBECK, COLIN L., JR. "Ars Gratia Artis." Commonweal,
      97 (17 November), 155.
      Review of Savage Messiah. Russell would like to be
      like Gaudier, oblivious of the world and in love with art
      for its own sake. He can't be like Gaudier, however, be-
      cause he prefers popularity and "his desire to be great is
      dissipated by his capacity to be mediocre."

320   _____. Review of The Boy Friend. Commonweal, 95 (7 January),
      326.
      Russell fails to make any real contrasts between the
      low-budget stage play and De Thrill's fantasies. The sets
      for each are equally elaborate, so everything stays on the
      same fairy-tale-like level.

321   WHITEHORN, ETHEL. "The Boy Friend." PTA Magazine, 66 (Feb-
      ruary), 36.
      Notice calls film "nostalgic, brightly entertaining."

322   _____. Notice of Savage Messiah. PTA Magazine, 67 (Decem-
      ber), 11.

323   WINOGURA, DALE. "The Devils." Cinefantastique, 2 (Spring),
      30-31.
      Film "exudes" Russell's personality. His earlier films,
      with the exception of The Music Lovers, were not suited to

his style. The Devils is his ideal subject and he portrays
the stifled, repressed, ignorant, superstitious seventeenth-
century masterfully. This film differs from other "offen-
sive" films such as The Loved One and Myra Breckinridge,
whose greatest offense is that they are "badly done" and
ill-conceived. Russell presents his intellectual nightmare
straightforwardly and significantly; the result is a "film
of unsurpassed power that reaches an abstract sublimity more
affecting and disturbing than any film made recently or pre-
viously."

324   ZIMMERMAN, PAUL D. "Portrait of the Artist." Newsweek, 80
      (20 November), 118-25.
          For the first time, in Savage Messiah, Russell succeeds
      in "communicating the white-hot energies of the creative
      act." His hero and heroine, with their "consuming love"
      for their art and their disregard of convention, resemble
      Russell himself.

                              1973

325   ANON. "Russell, Ken." In Celebrity Register. Edited by
      Earl Blackwell. New York: Simon and Schuster, p. 422.
          Brief piece stresses sensationalism surrounding Rus-
      sell and his work.

326   ANON. "Savage Messiah." Show, 2 (February), 53.
          Notice calls film "at once passionate farce and sensi-
      tive romance."

327   ARMSTRONG, DICK. "Ken Russell's Savage Messiah." Westport
      Trucker [Kansas City, Missouri], 3 (5 January), 12.
          Although not on a level with Russell's previous films,
      this is his most revealing and most autobiographical film.
      It is flawed but still inspired.

328   BAXTER, JOHN [and Ken Russell]. An Appalling Talent: Ken
      Russell. London: Michael Joseph, 240 pp.
          Fannish, incomplete, but entertaining study. Baxter's
      chapters deal mostly with his own experiences with Russell
      during the filming of Savage Messiah. He digresses for
      quotes from Huw Weldon, Russell's mentor at the BBC, and
      Dorothy Tutin, Sophie Brzeska in Savage Messiah. Russell's
      chapters are lively commentaries on his life and work. He
      discusses his work thoroughly; there is a rare discussion
      of his BBC films. His anecdotes throughout are highly
      entertaining. Filmography and index follow the text. See
      No. 377.

1973

329   BETTS, ERNEST. "Ken Russell." In his The Film Business: A
      History of British Cinema 1896-1972. New York, Toronto,
      and London: Pitman Publishing Corporation, pp. 306-311.
          Sketch of Russell's TV career. Discussions of Women in
      Love, The Music Lovers and The Devils and the reactions
      they provoked.

330   CARE, ROSS. "Ken Russell's The Devils--A Vivid Epic of Hor-
      ror." Lancaster Independent Press, 5 (13 April), 8, 10.
          Slightly altered version of No. 120.

331   CUFF, HASLETT. "The Devils." Georgia Straight [Vancouver,
      Canada], 7 (17 May), 14.
          Notice.

332   _____. "Ken Russell: Master or Magician?" Georgia Straight
      [Vancouver, Canada], 7 (8 November), 14-15.
          Savage Messiah is beautiful and touching, although it
      could have been sad, fruitless, trite or sentimental.
      "Blood, wisdom and savage despair ooze from the incredibly
      beautiful cinematography."

333   DEMPSEY, MICHAEL. "Savage Messiah." Film Heritage, 9 (Win-
      ter 1973/74), 9-16.
          Film is "beautiful tragicomedy" which differs in tone
      from earlier films in that it lacks "antiromantic satire,"
      the theme of transcendence, and Russell's usual attitude
      toward death. In it he "demystifies" the act of creating
      art--as Gaudier wished to do--without "deromanticizing"
      it. The first draft script shows some ambiguities which
      are eliminated in the film--Sophie's attitude toward Hen-
      ri's enlistment in the army is one of them.

334   FALTYSOVÁ, HELENA. "5/hf." Film a Doba, 19 (January), 8-9.
          Review of Savage Messiah which draws on Buckley, No.
      225. In Czech.

335   FARBER, STEPHEN. "Savage Messiah." Cinema [U.S.], 8 (Spring),
      40-41.
          Characterizes Russell's recurring theme as "beauty
      seized from the jaws of death"; it is illustrated in this
      film by the sequence in which Henri sculpts the tombstone.
      This is an "exuberant" film, Russell's most "accessible
      and seductive," but it ends with some "unsettling questions"
      about the ultimate purpose of art.

*336 FOX, TERRY CURTIS. "Conversations with Ken Russell." Oui
      (June), pp. 63-64, 102-108.
          [Cited in Gomez, No. 578, p. 217.]

337   GOMEZ, JOSEPH A. "Dante's Inferno: Seeing Ken Russell Through
       Dante Gabriel Rossetti." Literature/Film Quarterly, 1
       (July).
            Dante's Inferno contains "the essence of the Russell
       vision and method." He finds Rossetti's main conflict--
       that between his chivalric idealism and his "highly sexed
       nature"--and uses it as a focus to "build his own vision."
       He immerses himself in the period--finding actors resembling
       his subjects, using their works of art. Symbolic objects,
       tableaux, settings repeat themselves cyclically.

338   HOFSESS, JOHN. "Savage Messiah." Macleans, 86 (January), 70.
            All Russell's "waist-high tributes" are fed by his "one
       insight, that sex is the great leveler." This film is a
       "grade-B melodrama."

339   KOLKER, ROBERT PHILLIP. "Ken Russell's Biopics: Grander and
       Gaudier." Film Comment, 9 (May/June), 42-45.
            Russell's approach to biography: the subject is taken
       from three angles--the historical person, the myth created
       by his art, and Russell's own view of the subject. These
       are played off one another. Savage Messiah is discussed.

340   LEDÓCHOWSKI, ALEKSANDER. "Zimne Ognie" [Golden Rain]. Kino,
       8 (July), 41-47.
            Discusses Russell's films from French Dressing to Savage
       Messiah. Thorough filmography. In Polish.

341   LEFÈVRE, RAYMOND. "Le Messie Sauvage." Image et Son, No.
       268 (February), pp. 119-21.
            In Savage Messiah, in spite of the expert camerawork,
       the design, the colors, "it is the performance of the
       actors which makes all the film's impact." In French.

342   LOCHTE, DICK [and Michael Caine]. "Michael Caine's Life
       Flashes Before Him." Los Angeles Free Press, 10 (26 Janu-
       ary), 10, 11, 24.
            Interview touches on Caine's work in Billion Dollar
       Brain.

343   MEZAN, PETER [and Ken Russell]. "Relax, It's Only a Ken Rus-
       sell Movie." Esquire, 79 (May), 169-71, 198-204.
            Russell is portrayed as a director of "inexplicably
       tantalizing junk." He deals in the "Romance of the Bad
       Trip," in the artist as "obsessive." The interview empha-
       sizes his eccentricity as he discusses his outlandish ideas
       for past, present, and future films.

*344 MOORE, HARRY T. "D. H. Lawrence and the Flicks." Literature/
       Film Quarterly, 1 (January), 3-11.
            Discusses Women in Love. [Cited in Gomez, No. 578, p.
       219.]

1973

345   RENAUD, TRISTAN. "Sage Messiah (Le Messie Sauvage)--Le Cre-
      puscule des Diables" [The Twilight of the Devils]. Cinéma,
      No. 173 (February), pp. 106-107.
          Reviews Savage Messiah in relation to other Russell
      films. In French.

*346 ROBBINS, FRED. "The Savage Russell." Gallery, (May), pp.
      105-106, 126-27.
          [Cited in Gomez, No. 578, p. 219.]

347   SCHEPELERN, PETER. "Ken Russell og Billedernes Retorik" [Ken
      Russell and the Rhetoric of Filmmaking]. Kosmorama, 19
      (May), 176-84.
          Complex critique of Russell's work up to Savage Messiah,
      dealing with some of his consistent underlying themes, such
      as his characters' search for, and reaction to, relation-
      ships. In Danish.

348   TESSIER, MAX. "Le Messie Sauvage." Écran, 12 (February),
      63-65.
          Discusses Russell's approach to biography and to art in
      this, his most sedate film since Women in Love. In French.

349   TURRONI, GIUSEPPE. "Messia Selvaggio." Filmcritica, 24 (Jan-
      uary/February), 53.
          Review of Savage Messiah. In Italian.

350   ZAMBRANO, ANA LAURA. "Women in Love: Counterpoint on Film."
      Literature/Film Quarterly, 1 (January), 46-54.
          Detailed discussion of filmic and literary parallels--
      symbols, themes, etc. Characters are analyzed with insight
      and clarity, as are Russell's versions of the major inci-
      dents in the book.

                              1974

351   ANON. "Film: Mahler als Neurotiker." Der Spiegel, 28 (15
      April), 113.
          Notice of Mahler. In German.

352   ANON. "Ken Russell's Mahler." Films and Filming, 20 (April),
      33-36.
          Photo preview.

353   ANON. Review of Mahler. Films and Filming, 20 (April), 8.
          Film is "engrossing," encompassing emotion, sadness and
      humor.

354   BILLINGTON, MICHAEL. Review of Mahler. Illustrated London
      News, 262 (June), 87.

The "ultimate justification" of Russell's musical biopics is that "they are based on a profound love of the subject" and expose audiences to the music. Some scenes are excessive, others haunting.

355 COLEMAN, JOHN. "A Load of Symbolics." New Statesman, 87 (5 April), 488.
Mahler is Russell's "largest aberration to date." His films tell too little about their subjects and too much about him. The film is loaded with symbols, some of which succeed visually--but Russell is "working too strenuously at it and slipping toward Hollywood values in the same bewildering instant."

356 DANSKY, JOEL. "Savage Messiah." Valley Advocate [Amherst, Massachusetts], 1 (20 February), 16-17.
Review.

357 DE LA GRANGE, HENRY-LOUIS. "L'Opinion du 'Mahlerien' No. 1 Sur L'Extravagant M. Russell." L'Express, No. 1192 (13 May), p. 107.
De La Grange, a Mahler scholar, praises Mahler's visual beauty, but deplores Russell's "reinvention" of the character. In French.

358 ELLEY, DEREK. "Mahler." Films and Filming, 20 (May), 41-43.
The film contains some of Russell's most brilliant work in terms of images and technical expertise, and also some of his "greatest hyperboles." He seems uncertain whether to go over the edge, as in the Strauss film, or, like the Delius, to be gentler and more accurate. Russell's skill in telescoping and interpolating events is discussed, along with his use of music.

359 GILLETT, JOHN. "Mahler." [BFI] Monthly Film Bulletin, 41 (April), 76-77.
Credits, synopsis, review. Some sequences are too far-out, some use music interestingly, others use it oddly, cutting the music to fit the images instead of the reverse.

360 GOW, GORDON. "Mahler." In International Film Guide 1975. Edited by Peter Cowie. London: Tantivy Press; New York: A. S. Barnes, pp. 153, 155.
Notice emphasizes the utterly filmic quality of Russell's style.

361 GREEN, BENNY. "Gustav Wind." Punch, 266 (17 April), 654.
In Mahler and other films, Russell's "mundane mind" and lack of musical perceptiveness are deplored, and his use

1974

of music to bring on fantasy sequences deflated--"very often
music doesn't 'mean' anything at all." He has talent; his
"posturings" are sometimes beautiful.

362   GREENFIELD, PIERRE. "Mahler." Take One, 4 (July), 28-30.
         Discussion of some of Russell's eccentric symbolism. His
unbounded egoism is seen as the vital force in this and
other films; each successive film exemplifies his artistic
development. His treatment of the Mahler-Alma relationship
is the most touching of his career, the development of
Mahler's character more careful than others. As an artist-
as-critic, Russell uses the film to assess not only Mahler
but his own earlier films.

363   HALL, WILLIAM. "What the Blazes is Ken Russell Up to Now?
A Rock Opera." New York Times (23 June), Section 2, pp.
13, 29.
         Interviews on the set of Tommy--mostly Russell--and
description of the filming of the "Blitz" sequence.

364   HALLIWELL, LESLIE. "Russell, Ken." In his The Filmgoer's
Companion. New York: Hill and Wang, p. 669.
         Film list.

365   HAWK. "Mahler." Variety, 274 (10 April), 17.
         Film is usual blend of "Russellian extremes," "vastly
uneven," but frequently brilliant in its perceptions of the
experience of being an artist.

366   HUDSON, CHRISTOPHER. "Mauling Mahler." Spectator, 232 (13
April), 456.
         "Russell knows how to direct actors and how to direct
cameras--it's putting them together that seems to defeat
him." Mahler is another of his "bargain basement intro-
ductions to the Classics."

367   LEFÈVRE, RAYMOND. "Mahler." Cinéma, No. 190-91 (September/
October), pp. 279-81.
         Discussion of Russell's recurring themes and images
(death, decomposition, insanity) and his methods (dream
sequences, farce, humor, horror, expressionistic and in-
teriorized treatment of biography) in relation to Mahler.

368   MANNS, TORSTEN. "Cannes XXVII." Chaplin, pp. 132-33.
         Notice of Mahler. In Swedish.

369   MILLAR, GAVIN. Review of Mahler. Listener, 91 (11 April), 481.
         Notice says that Russell's gift is "literalness in
imagery" which produces both puns and vulgarity. Mahler
has both, although it has very little to do with Mahler
himself.

370   MORAVIA, ALBERTO. "Le Gesta d'Un Ebreo Qualsiasi" [The
       Achievement of an Ordinary Jew]. L'Espresso, No. 22 (2
       June), pp. 86-87.
          Mahler is dealt with mainly as a study of the composer's
       Jewishness. In Italian.

371   PERRY, GEORGE. "Ken Russell." In his The Great British Pic-
       ture Show. New York: Hill and Wang, pp. 274-75, 332-33.
          Brief survey of Russell's feature film career; filmo-
       graphical listing.

372   POWELL, DILYS. "Music Lover." Sunday Times [London], (7
       April), p. 37.
          Certain passages of Mahler produce "delighted admiration"
       and prove that Russell is no mediocre creator. Consider-
       ing the combination of delicate mood and gross excess,
       Russell is a "frightening and preposterous" mixture of "Ben-
       jamin Robert Haydon, Hieronymus Bosch, and the propaganda-
       poster artists of the Third Reich."

373   PREVIN, ANDRE [and Ken Russell]. "Andre Previn Meets Ken Rus-
       sell." Listener, 92 (19 September), 367.
          Interview concerns Russell's feelings toward, and use
       of, music.

374   QUIRK, LAWRENCE J. "The Music Lovers." In his The Great Ro-
       mantic Films. Secaucus, New Jersey: Citadel Press, pp.
       200-203.
          Credits, photos. Film is "individualistic, gorgeously
       sensual, hyper-cruel, racily uninhibited"; although the
       film is odd, it is always interesting. Russell doesn't
       exaggerate the "essentials" of Tchaikovsky's lifestyle.

375   REED, REX. "On Location: Ken Russell." In his People Are
       Crazy Here. New York: Dell, pp. 251-56.
          Article written during the filming of The Boy Friend
       shows Russell as a raving megalomaniacal loudmouth.

376   ROBINSON, DAVID. "Poor Mahler Gets the Russell Treatment."
       The Times [London] (5 April), p. 9.
          Russell seems to be "mellowing" with Mahler; despite his
       "distaste" for his subjects, he manages some "gentle charm"
       in his treatment of Alma Mahler.

377   SIMON, JOHN. "Citizen Ken." Times Literary Supplement [Lon-
       don] (8 November), p. 1253.
          Discussion of Russell in relation to the Baxter book,
       No. 328. Critique of the book itself.

1974

378   TAURUS. "Is Ken Russell Into Black Magic?" <u>Other Scenes</u>
      [Cannes], n.p.
          Russell's films seem to show that he is acquainted with
      the various aspects of Satanism.

379   TESSIER, MAX. "<u>Mahler</u>." <u>Écran</u>, 30 (November), 61-62.
          Review, closing with the provisory opinion that Russell
      is a sort of cinematic vampire, living off the flesh and
      blood of the artists he immortalizes. Cast and credits
      list. In French.

380   WALKER, ALEXANDER. "Fantasists: Boorman, Russell." In his
      <u>Hollywood U. K.</u> New York: Stein and Day, pp. 383-92.
          Russell's section of the subchapter (pp. 387-92) analy-
      zes his strengths and weaknesses. Several films are
      mentioned in passing; <u>Women in Love</u> is discussed more
      thoroughly. Russell is a genius at capturing historical
      detail and positioning figures in the frame to create
      special effects, but he is also sometimes vulgar and banal.

*381 WALKER, JOHN. "Ken Russell's New Enigma." <u>Observer Magazine</u>
      [London] (8 September), pp. 51-53, 55, 57.
          [Cited in <u>British Humanities Index 1974</u>, p. 390.]

382   WILSON, COLIN. <u>Ken Russell: A Director in Search of a Hero</u>.
      London: Intergroup Publishing, 71 pp.
          This essay in book form offers the author's highly
      personal view of Russell's films and ideas, as well as
      some biographical and career information supplied by
      Wilson's BBC interview with Russell. Elegantly laid-out
      and illustrated.

                              1975

383   ALPERT, HOLLIS. "The Murder of Mahler." <u>Saturday Review</u>, 2
      (8 February), 39.
          Russell's attempts at portraying the creative mind and
      the creative process are an all-too-thinly disguised ex-
      pression of his own ego, in <u>Mahler</u> and other films. In
      this one, his "symbolism" is heavyhanded and his "im-
      pressionistic" methods are an excuse for distortion of
      facts. Certain elements, such as the introduction of
      Nazism into the story, make no sense.

384   _____. "Puzzles and Pop." <u>Saturday Review</u>, 2 (3 May), 35.
          <u>Tommy</u> is bemusing, the images are Russell's "hallucina-
      tions."

385   ANKENBRANDT, THOMAS F., S.J.   "Tommy as Glittering Messiah."
       National Catholic Reporter [Kansas City, Missouri] (9 May).
           Film is "a proclamation of the gospel of excess"; it
       illustrates the effect of commercialization on everything
       important (including religion)--man finds that the thing
       he worships is worthless.   [NB, Card 37.]

386   ANON.   "Ann-Margret: Survival."   Dallas Morning News (23
       March).
           Article with interview excerpts, mostly concerning
       Tommy.   [NB, Card 25.]

387   ANON.   "The Dark Brilliance of Ken Russell."   New York Daily
       News (30 March).
           Contrasts Russell's flamboyant reputation with the man
       himself.   Discusses the development of Tommy, using quotes
       from Russell, and touches on his approaches to other films.
       [NB, Card 23.]

388   ANON.   "Film Version of Tommy Lives Up to Its Promise."   Bos-
       ton Globe (27 March).
           Russell's "total ignorance of the rock scene" may be the
       greatest contributing factor to the film's success.   He
       uses metaphor, symbol and picture to produce a film that
       "roars."   [NB, Card 26.]

389   ANON.   "Ken Russell's Lisztomania."   Films and Filming, 22
       (November), 26-31.
           Picture preview.

390   ANON.   "Lisztomania."   Playboy, 22 (October), 84-89.
           Lurid photo preview.

391   ANON.   "Mahler."   Lot's Wife [Melbourne, Australia], 15 (4
       March), 13.
           Russell seems to equate "the flouting of convention with
       artistic merit"; his film contains some outrageous scenes,
       but they are also banal and cliché-ridden, and shed no light
       on Mahler himself.

392   ANON.   "Opera Tommy No Barber of Seville."   Arizona Republic
       [Phoenix] (27 March).
           Film will appeal mostly to younger people, though it
       is an interesting experience for all.   Some of the "arias"
       don't work but others are potent.   [NB, Card 25.]

393   ANON.   "Pre-Search."   Film Bulletin, 44 (January), 14-24.
           Exhaustive analysis of Tommy's sales potential.

1975

394   ANON. Review of <u>Mahler</u>. <u>Playboy</u>, 22 (April), 42, 44.
      "Messy," "gaudy" film "clinches Russell's nomination
      for a 1975 Snafu Award as the director most likely to
      fall on his ass with flair."

395   ANON. "Rich Success Fails Here." <u>Richmond Times-Dispatch</u>
      [Virginia] (16 November).
      <u>Lisztomania</u> is original, fascinating and humorous, with
      enjoyable performances, but it somehow fails to draw large
      audiences. [<u>NB</u>, Card 73.]

396   ANON. "Rock Film <u>Tommy</u>: 'Ich bin eine Sensation.'" <u>Der
      Spiegel</u>, 29 (21 April), 142, 145.
      Background article. In German.

397   ANON. "<u>Tommy</u>." <u>Films and Filming</u>, 21 (March), 51-56.
      Photo preview.

398   ANON. "<u>Tommy</u>." <u>Take Over</u> [Madison], 5 (24 April), 14.
      Film is a "feast for the eyes," a "pleasure for the
      ears," and a "lobotomy for the brain."

399   ANON. "<u>Tommy</u>--A Massive Assault on the Senses." <u>Journal Star</u>
      [Peoria, Illinois] (18 May).
      Russell has turned "silk purses into sows' ears" before
      (such as <u>The Music Lovers</u>), but he's never done it "with
      such ostentation, with such dramatic overkill." <u>Tommy</u> is
      "all peak and no valley," incoherent due to the "inarticu-
      late resentment of the 1960's" whence the work sprung. It
      is "slightly mad in a ghastly, garish, neon, glittery,
      wonderful and repulsive way." [<u>NB</u>, Card 37.]

400   ANON. "<u>Tommy</u> Complex, But Not Confusing." <u>Metro-East Journal</u>
      [East St. Louis, Illinois] (27 April).
      "<u>Tommy</u> will last"--it raises questions not usually
      approached in popular films in a memorable way. [<u>NB</u>, Card
      26.]

401   ANON. "<u>Tommy</u> Frantic, Savage, Excessive and Fascinating."
      <u>Miami Herald</u> (11 April).
      Russell's style is more suited to <u>Tommy</u> than to his past
      subjects. It is a mix of "childlike plot devices," and
      "sophisticated thinking" which gets in some good shots at
      pop culture. Its main fault is that it "starts to climax
      six or seven times" before it ends. [<u>NB</u>, Card 25.]

402   ANON. "<u>Tommy</u> Is Genuine Rock Opera." <u>Indianapolis Star</u> (28
      March).
      The film is the "nearest approach" to real opera to hit
      the screen so far. It is relentless in its energy--so much
      so that individual parts have more impact than the whole.
      [<u>NB</u>, Card 26.]

403   ANON. "Tommy Stuns the Senses." Florida Times Union [Jack-
        sonville] (1 June).
            The film is a "high-powered visual trip" whose "ultimate
        point doesn't really matter very much." It is "altogether
        overwhelming." [NB, Card 37.]

404   ANON. "Tommy to the Rescue." Films and Filming, 21 (April),
        10.
            Pre-release background article, listing some memorable
        moments in the film, and expressing hope that it will re-
        vitalize the British cinema.

405   ANON. "What's Deaf, Dumb and Blind and Costs $3 1/2 Million?
        Tommy." Rolling Stone, No. 184 (10 April), pp. 44-46.
            Article discusses film's pre-release promotion; its con-
        ceptualization according to Russell and Townshend; plot
        synopsis, background information.

406   ANONYMOUS ATAVISTIC ARCHEOPTERYX. "Archeopteryx at the Flix."
        Great Speckled Bird [Atlanta], 8 (13 November), 14.
            There are some brilliant moments in Lisztomania, but
        after a while the continual "freak show" loses its power
        to shock.

407   ANSEN, DAVID. "Culture Porn." Real Paper [Boston], 4 (29
        October), 30.
            Russell's schizoid treatment of romanticism--at once
        satirical and indulgent--gave his better films their odd
        fascination. This balance is gone in Lisztomania; the
        lunacy is untempered by Russell's usual insight and allows
        no humanity.

408   ARNOLD, GARY. "A Lewd Liszt to a Rock Beat." Washington Post
        (24 October), Section B, p. 10.
            In Lisztomania, Russell is long on visual and technical
        brilliance but appallingly short on control and intellectual
        imagination.

409   _____. "Tommy: Now a Film." Washington Post (27 March),
        Section C, pp. 1, 13.
            Russell's scenario is "draggy, heavily melodramatized."
        The libretto was better when more obscure. Russell is
        guilty of dramatic overkill in making every number so
        "splashy."

410   ARNOLD, JAMES. "A Phenomenon Called Tommy." Milwaukee Jour-
        nal Insight (18 May), pp. 36-37.
            Film is, "for good or bad...the ultimate cinema experi-
        ence in sensuality." Film has a natural affinity to music;
        their potential impact when combined has only been sporadi-

1975

cally explored in works like <u>Woodstock</u>, <u>2001</u>, and <u>Fantasia</u>.
<u>Tommy</u> is the first "rock" movie because unlike the similar
<u>Jesus Christ Superstar</u> and <u>Godspell</u>, it has an "entirely
original <u>visual</u> libretto." Russell's satirical sense is
illustrated by several sequences in the film.

411 ATLAS, JACOBA. "Close, But No Cigar." <u>Los Angeles Free Press</u>,
12 (18 April), 19, 20.
The film of <u>Tommy</u> bears little resemblance to the original opera; it changes the focus of Tommy's discovery of
divinity from man to God, thus altering the Who's conception. The photography and direction ranges from brilliant
to childish, and most of the cast is wasted.

412 _____. "<u>Mahler</u>." <u>Los Angeles Free Press</u>, 12 (21 February),
19, 21.
Mahler is a perfect subject for Russell. The relationship between the composer and his wife is interestingly
portrayed and there are many joking references both to
Mahler and to Russell's earlier films.

413 BANKS, DICK. "Hard on the Heels of <u>Tommy</u>, <u>Lisztomania</u> Is Too
Much." <u>Charlotte Observer</u> [North Carolina] (10 November).
Review. [<u>NB</u>, Card 73.]

414 _____. "Lovely Ann-Margret Spices Rock-Filled <u>Tommy</u> Cast."
<u>Charlotte Observer</u> [North Carolina] (24 May).
Film is youthful, exuberant, but overlong; Ann-Margret's
performance is outstanding. [<u>NB</u>, Card 37.]

415 BANNON, ANTHONY. "<u>Tommy</u> Transcends the Radical in Frantic
Assault on Convention." <u>Buffalo Evening News</u> [New York]
(27 March).
Short review discusses film's flamboyant innovativeness
and its actors' performances. [<u>NB</u>, Card 26.]

416 BARTON, SUSAN. "<u>Tommy</u>! <u>Tommy</u>! <u>Tommy</u>!" <u>American-Statesman</u>
[Austin, Texas] (23 March).
Review and account of incidents at film's sneak preview
in Dallas, and quotes by Ann-Margret about the filming.
[<u>NB</u>, Card 25.]

417 BASCH, RICHARD. "The Living Arts." <u>Chicago Tribune Tuesday
Magazine</u> (8 June), p. 14.
Short review calls <u>Tommy</u> a "film of sweep and overwhelm-
ing power," praising in particular the performance of Tina
Turner.

418 BATCHELOR, RUTH. "A Classic of the 70's?" <u>Los Angeles Free
Press</u>, 12 (18 April), 18.

The bizarre touches that Russell adds to the Tommy
story--the Monroe religion, the Cousin Kevin sequence--
have a sort of cockeyed moral purpose. Although the director borrows from the avant-garde filmmakers, he also
has his own, ever-growing style. Tommy is not a film to
"like" or "dislike"; like the seventies, "it is here and
we should live through it."

419   BATCHELOR, RUTH [and Ken and Shirley Russell]. "Shirley and
      Ken (Tommy) Russell on Fashion, Film and Mountains." Los
      Angeles Free Press, 12 (19 September), 22, 27.
            The Russells also discuss their reactions to Los Angeles
      and other directors.

420   BATDORFF, EMERSON. "Rocking Tommy Causes Ache in Teeth Over
      50." Plain Dealer [Cleveland] (27 March).
            Film is enjoyable, but would be more so if the sound
      were less shattering. The philosophy of the film is "it
      is unwise to trust people in the generation that pays the
      bills." [NB, Card 26.]

421   BEAN, ROBIN. "Lenny and the Rock Age Heroes." Films and Film-
      ing, 22 (December), 48.
            Review of the soundtrack LP of Tommy; it is "devastat-
      ing."

422   _____. "Tommy." Films and Filming, 21 (May), 34-35.
            Film is a "milestone in British cinema"; hopefully it
      will revive British filmmaking, plagued by widespread de-
      fection of artists to the States and elsewhere. Russell
      remains "subservient" to the material, providing extra-
      ordinary images and a nearly faultless cast.

423   BENJAMIN, ERIC. "Tommy." Valley Advocate [Amherst, Massachu-
      setts], 1 (17 April), 18, 19.
            Film is the best rock movie ever, "for the first time
      combining many different media into one working artistic
      synthesis."

424   BUTLER, ROBERT W. "Russell's Tommy: Glorious Audacity."
      Kansas City Star [Missouri] (30 March).
            Film is the "most glorious, eccentric, memorable failure
      in years"; it is the first film in which Russell's material
      matches his style. One problem is that most performers
      are either singers or actors, not both. Another is that
      the opera's ambiguous "message"--which can be interpreted
      differently by each listener--becomes too literal onscreen.
      [NB, Card 26.]

97

1975

425 BUTLER, RONALD C. "Viewpoint." <u>Tulsa World</u> (27 April).
     <u>Tommy</u> is "painfully long, annoyingly repetitious" and
     unsatisfying for sophisticated audiences. There are some
     imaginative, powerful scenes when Russell "somehow gets
     that strange realm of his mind onto film." [<u>NB</u>, Card 26.]

426 CALLOWAY, EARL. "<u>Tommy</u> Overpowering." <u>Daily Defender</u> [Chica-
     go] (27 March).
     The opera is "musically stagnant"; some vocal perform-
     ances are poor, some isolated moments are good. [<u>NB</u>, Card
     26.]

427 CANBY, VINCENT. "Film: <u>Tommy</u>, the Who's Rock Saga." <u>New
     York Times</u> (20 March), p. 48.
     Russell's methods are always spectacular--dizzying turns,
     falls, changes--but until now this treatment has seemed
     "wickedly foolish." In <u>Tommy</u> it "liberates" the over-
     serious story.

428 _____. "When Too Much Is Just About Right." <u>New York Times</u>
     (30 March), Section 2, p. 13.
     In contrast to Russell's other "gargantuan mistakes,"
     his heavyhandedness fits <u>Tommy</u>. It "captures the spectacu-
     lar tastelessness of an era" as its "overindulgence ap-
     proaches art."

429 CARROLL, KATHLEEN. "<u>Tommy</u>--It Gluts." <u>New York Daily News</u>
     (19 March), p. 68.
     The film's one-dimensionality disappoints; it also lets
     down the Townshend score.

430 CASTELL, DAVID. "<u>Lisztomania</u>." <u>Films Illustrated</u>, 5 (Novem-
     ber), 100-101.
     Russell "spews forth" ideas, many of which fail, and
     many of which are very vulgar. The film is not great, but
     deserves serious consideration. Note on Russell follows
     review.

431 _____. "<u>Tommy</u>." <u>Films Illustrated</u>, 4 (April), 286.
     Film has "extraordinary raw power" although its plot is
     "hackneyed." It weakens when Tommy is cured, but is car-
     ried along by its own inertia. Some sequences are disturb-
     ing. Followed by notes on rock opera and Quintaphonic
     sound.

432 _____ [and Roger Daltrey]. "Daltrey's Good Vibrations."
     <u>Films Illustrated</u>, 4 (April), 300-302.
     Article/interview deals largely with <u>Tommy</u> and <u>Liszto-
     mania</u>.

433 CHARLESWORTH, STEPHEN. "Pete Saves Tommy." Farrago [Moonee
     Ponds, Australia], 53 (17 April), 24.
        Most of the credit for the film goes to Townshend rather
     than Russell, since it is an "acted working out of the
     songs" rather than a totally original scenario.

434 COCKS, JAY. "Tommy Rocks In." Time, 105 (31 March), 56-59.
        The subject "invites and requires" visual absurdity.
     As a filmmaker, Russell is fearless, with disregard for
     both taste and fact. He satirizes the seriousness of the
     acceptance of the rock opera itself, but only "exposes but
     does not defeat" its "daffy banality." Background infor-
     mation and coverage of the film's New York premiere subway
     party.

435 COHN, NIK. Review of Lisztomania. New Times, 5 (12 December),
     65.
        Quotes the soundtrack album's vulgar liner notes as
     indicative of the film's "cosmic God-awfulness," and charac-
     terizes Russell as a forty-year-old bedwetting brat.

436 COLEMAN, JOHN. "Quintaphonic Ken." New Statesman, 89 (28
     March), 425.
        The sound system used for Tommy is an "aural affront"--
     but Tommy is essentially a silent movie. Russell has
     "mercifully loose foundations" here on which to build his
     fantasies--at least he isn't "bending a real biography."
     He is allowed some extraordinary visuals, so many that the
     film is more Joycean than Strick's Ulysses. He uses the
     medium as almost no filmmaker has before. Tommy is "the
     film many of us suspected, and some of us feared, Mr.
     Russell always had in him."

437 ____. "Transfer Liszt." New Statesman, 90 (14 November),
     622-23.
        Russell's relationship with musical biography is that
     of "a rapist with a victim." Lisztomania is incoherent
     throughout and looks like the end of Russell's odd bril-
     liance as a director.

438 CRIST, JUDITH. Notice of Lisztomania. Saturday Review, 3
     (29 November), 38.
        Film is "an ordeal for any but Ken Russell maniacs."

439 ____. "Opera On the Rocks, With a Twist." New York, 8 (7
     April), 64-65.
        Russell and Tommy "serve each other well." Although the
     opera's philosophy is "mush minded," the visual and aural
     onslaught is stunning and sometimes numbing.

1975

440   CUFF, HASLETT. "Lisztomania: Glitter and Grand Guignol."
       Georgia Straight [Vancouver, Canada], 9 (30 October), 15.
            The film is offensive even to Russell fans; it contains
       none of the fine acting and effective use of music that dis-
       tinguish his better films. His dislike of Wagner is becom-
       ing "very tiresome."

441   _____. "Romantic Dementia, Art as Hallucination." Georgia
       Straight [Vancouver, Canada], 9 (27 March), 8.
            In Mahler, Russell explores the composer's "dreamlife"
       in a series of beautiful, striking images and a set of good
       performances by his actors. The film is "exasperating";
       it thrills and moves; its ending is trite but at the same
       time "a gratefully received affirmation of your most roman-
       tic expectations."

442   _____. "Tommy!" Georgia Straight [Vancouver, Canada], 9 (17
       April), 8.
            The film bores, leaves no impression, despite Russell's
       efforts to elevate the undistinguished rock opera and the
       fine performances of his cast.

443   CUSKELLY, RICHARD. "War Baby Tommy." Los Angeles Herald
       Examiner (20 March).
            Tommy, along with M*A*S*H, The Godfather and Shampoo,
       is one of the most innovative films of the past few years.
       [NB, Card 25.]

444   CUTLER, HUGH. "Tommy Translates to Film as Sight, Sound Ex-
       travaganza." Wilmington Evening Journal (28 June).
            Film is too extravagant for the opera's philosophy to
       be taken seriously. It is "psychedelic fluff," but none-
       theless "dazzling." [NB, Card 37.]

445   DAMSKER, MATT. "Tommy: From Vinyl to Film." Evening Bulle-
       tin [Philadelphia] (23 March).
            Review and short history of Tommy, from original record
       to film. [NB, Card 26.]

446   DAVIS, PETER G. "Ken Russell's Film Studies of Composers--
       Brilliance Gone Berserk." New York Times (19 October),
       Section 2, pp. 1, 13.
            Mourns Russell's "sad decline", comparing the "trivial,
       irrelevant and unswervingly stupid" Lisztomania with his
       earlier Mahler, Tchaikovsky and Delius films, all of which
       possess originality of image, thought and feeling that the
       Liszt film totally lacks. See No. 509.

447   DOHERTY, JAMES J. "Tommy is Movie That Tunes In." News and
       Courier [Charleston, South Carolina] (22 June).

Humorous account of author's first exposure to the
original album followed by a review which finds the film
adolescent but "fun." [NB, Card 37.]

448   EBERT, ROGER. "Tommy's Too Much." Chicago Sun Times (24
      March).
      Film is "a case of glorious overkill" which works be-
      cause "it never stops for a breath or a second thought."
      It is a bit too long and exhausting. [NB, Card 26.]

449   EDER, RICHARD. "Lisztomania." New York Times (11 October),
      p. 23.
      Film is a "tiny, potentially appealing weed of a pic-
      ture," which begins hilariously but becomes pretentious
      as well as ludicrous.

450   EDWARDS, HENRY. "Preview with Pictures: Tommy Rocks the
      Silver Screen." After Dark, 7 (February), 52-56.
      Pictures and background on the Who and the film, followed
      by an article on Ann-Margret.

451   EDWARDS, JOE. "Liszto-Blitzo." Aquarian [Montclair, New
      Jersey], 10 (22 October), 33.
      The overbudgeted, overindulged Lisztomania is uniformly
      awful, a biographical "fraud," and a musical perversion.

452   _____. "Tommy: Hype or Art?" Aquarian [Montclair, New
      Jersey], 10 (9 April), 12, 29.
      The film's commercial success is causing it to be over-
      looked as the work of art it is. There are several flaws
      in it, but the worst aspect of the film is really the
      merchandising hype that accompanies it.

453   FARBER, STEPHEN. "Russellmania." Film Comment, 11 (Novem-
      ber/December), 40-47.
      Long, complex analysis examines Russell's works as they
      express his themes of "art snatched from the jaws of death"
      and "the artist's ruthlessness in pursuing his vision"--
      the films that do not deal with these seem "less urgent."
      Discusses Russell's ambivalence toward "hard-edged women"--
      a "combination of fascination and suspicion" which may not
      make his women sympathetic, but makes them strong charac-
      ters. Tommy and Lisztomania share a "circus"-type style
      and a lack of emotional rapport, although the latter film
      is the more inventive and reflects Russell's themes; he
      "still envisions art as the central creative act that brings
      order to a chaotic universe." As a filmmaker, his flaws
      are a lack of "warmth and compassion," an indifferent ear
      for dialog. His "arrogance, self-indulgence, pomposity
      and sensationalism" may be his strengths, as they often
      are among film directors.

1975

454 FELDMAN, SYLVIA. "<u>Tommy</u>." <u>Human Behavior</u>, 4 (July), 77.
      The film is "a case history of craziness, beginning with
      the etiology of the disorder" which "culminates with a
      psychotic solution in which the patient is made godlike
      and free from the suffering of his pilloried body."

455 FELTON, JAMES. "Facts Distorted in Rock 'Bio' of Composer."
      <u>Evening Bulletin</u> [Philadelphia] (1 November).
      <u>Lisztomania</u> is "far sillier than anything that can be
      said about it." Review deals mostly with the music and
      Russell's and Wakeman's use of it. [<u>NB</u>, Card 73.]

456 FORBES, CHERYL. "Pinball Trivia." <u>Christianity Today</u>, 19 (6
      June), 21-22.
      Review of <u>Tommy</u> emphasizing the grotesqueries, es-
      pecially the use of established church rituals and Tom-
      my's messianic claims as parody.

457 FOX, THOMAS. "<u>Tommy</u> Can Be Fun, But Tests Endurance." <u>Com-
      mercial Appeal</u> [Memphis] (3 May).
      Film is "a very good time," but its length is tiring.
      [<u>NB</u>, Card 37.]

458 GAGNARD, FRANK. "<u>Tommy</u> Meets Ken Russell." <u>Times-Picayune</u>
      [New Orleans] (29 March).
      Parts of the film reach "soaring brilliance" although
      there is the usual Russellian "garbage-wallowing." Faults
      are the need to maintain images for the length of the songs,
      some blasphemous moments, and outmoded psychedelic effects.
      [<u>NB</u>, Card 26.]

459 GAINES, STEVEN. "What's All This <u>Tommy</u> Rot?" <u>New York Daily
      News</u> (16 March), p. 11.
      Preview of the film based on pre-release hype and the
      soundtrack album.

460 GALLIGAN, RICHARD. Review of <u>Lisztomania</u>. <u>New Haven Register</u>
      [Connecticut] (2 November).
      The film is a "bloated bore." In theory its ideas are
      clever; in actuality "they play like burlesque routines in
      a slaughterhouse." [<u>NB</u>, Card 73.]

461 _____. "<u>Tommy</u> Is...Like Wow!" <u>New Haven Register</u> [Connecti-
      cut] (13 April).
      The film besieges the audience--much like Russell's
      earlier works, but this time it's the right approach.
      One of the film's pluses is Russell's explorations of the
      music. [<u>NB</u>, Card 25.]

462 GALLO, WILLIAM. "Ken Russell Scores a Triumph with <u>Tommy</u>."
      <u>Rocky Mountain News</u> [Denver] (25 April).

102

This is "Russell's best film"; it gives him a chance to exercise his taste for the grotesque. At the same time, it is his "most disciplined film." [NB, Card 25.]

463 GARDNER, R. H. "Not Liszt But Critic-o-Mania in Film." Sun [Baltimore] (10 November).
Lisztomania has little substance and much tastelessness. Russell has talent, but he is "squandering" it. [NB, Card 68.]

464 _____. "Tommy Has One Note: Frenzy." Sun [Baltimore] (13 April).
Treatment is right for material--"Tommy treated serious-ly might have been a mess." There is repetitiveness of dramatic effect among the separate sequences, but also "inspiration and inventiveness." [NB, Card 26.]

465 GEORGES. "Mahler de Ken Russell." Mainmise [Montreal], No. 48, p. 33.
Review. In French.

466 _____. "Tommy de Ken Russell." Mainmise [Montreal], No. 49, p. 48.
Review. In French.

467 GERBER, ERIC. "Film: Tommy." Houston Post (27 March).
Russell's fusion of sound and image is admirable. Tommy is "the film Cocteau would make if he liked rock and roll." [NB, Card 26.]

468 GILLIATT, PENELOPE. "Tommy." New Yorker, 51 (7 April), 123-24.
Humorous Platonic dialog review in which Aging-Fad raves about Tommy in current jargon while Against protests that the film is shallow, excessive, and the epitome of the commercialism it purportedly satirizes. He points out that fearlessness isn't always synonymous with goodness in art. Tommy embodies "a greedy epoch of no grace."

469 GOMEZ, JOSEPH A. "Mahler and the Methods of Ken Russell's Films on Composers." Velvet Light Trap, No. 14 (Winter) pp. 45-50.
Goes back to Russell's earliest TV films: Elgar, Bar-tok, The Debussy Film, Song of Summer, Dance of the Seven Veils--and The Music Lovers--and traces the development of his style in which music becomes an organic part of the film and in which time, space, fact, myth, psychology and symbol all together take the place of narrative and expo-sition. Russell's approach to Mahler is closely analyzed.

1975

470 GREEN, BENNY. "Shoot the Pianist." Punch, 267 (19 November),
952.
A short dissertation on the sex appeal of musicians is
followed by reviews of The Loves of Liszt and Lisztomania,
"each more asinine than the other." The former is a cliché-
ridden, badly dubbed conventional biopic, while Russell's
is one of a series of "bad jokes," perhaps "the silliest
picture ever made by a gifted man."

471 HALL, KEITH, JR. "Tommy." Sun Rise [Macomb, Illinois], 4,
No. 1, p. 51.
Russell often sets up scenes promisingly, but ultimately
"beats his moments to death." When his images and the
music work together, the film is "near brilliant," but this
happens only a few times.

472 HARDAWAY, FRANCINE. "Tommy." New Times [Tempe, Arizona], 6
(2 April), 16.
The film is "exhilarating and exhausting." The cast is
terrific, and Russell's imagination is "endless."

473 HENSCHEN, BOB. "Tommy." New Times [Tempe, Arizona], 6 (2
April), 16, 20.
Film is "excellent" in all respects; even the heavy-
handed symbolism has a function. The cast is good, the
scenery and photography unique.

474 HEUMAN, SCOTT. "Lisztomania." Iconoclast [Dallas], 9 (31
October), 14.
The film is another step in Russell's decline, self-
indulgent, silly, and "manic."

475 HODENFIELD, J. "See Me--Feel Me--Touch Me." New York Post
(21 March).
Tommy is "sort of a good movie." The music is not good,
but what Russell does with it is. It is odd that the film
seems to attack the "urban, lower class, technological"
roots from which British rock sprung. Discusses the New
York premiere party. [NB, Card 26.]

476 HOFSESS, JOHN. "This Deaf, Dumb and Blind Kid Has No Class."
Macleans, 88 (June), 84.
Tommy is "monumentally silly," with "bad, loud music"
and "anachronistic theology." Russell as a director promises much more than he ever delivers; he "pussyfoots."

477 HOGNER, STEVE. "Russell's Mahler: An Undismissable Failure."
American-Statesman [Austin, Texas] (15 February).
The film is memorable, expressionistic, visually stunning.
There is too much of Russell's personal symbolism and dis-
tracting in-jokes. One of the film's strengths is its good
cast. [NB, Card 26.]

478 HUDDY, JOHN. "Tommy." Miami Herald (13 April).
     Review praises visuals and harsh messages of some se-
     quences, calls film a "caricature of a caricature." In-
     cludes quotes from Townshend, Tina Turner, and Ann-Margret
     concerning their reactions to the finished film. [NB,
     Card 26.]

479 INMAN, RICK. "Lisztomania: 'Smut, Blasphemy,' But No Per-
     version." Bugle American [Milwaukee], 6 (3 December), 36.
     Takes issue with the Legion of Decency's condemnation
     of the film.

480 ____. "Russell's Latest Mania--List." Bugle American [Mil-
     waukee], 6 (12 November), 22-23.
     Lisztomania is "repulsive," alienating, unsympathetic.

481 ____. "Tommy." Bugle American [Milwaukee], 6 (16 April),
     17, 18.
     Film is "obnoxious, utterly offensive." The original
     work was hopeful, promoting the "nobility of man"; its
     music was "primitive" but vital. Russell's version is a
     "cinematic smirk," drenched in vulgarity.

482 JOHNSON, MALCOLM L. "Russell's Tommy." Hartford Courant
     [Connecticut] (13 April).
     Film is a "highly enjoyable pop masterwork," although
     Russell labors the obvious and is sometimes too literal in
     matching words to images. The "symbolic" killing of Tom-
     my's father is "made to seem" literal. [NB, Card 25.]

483 KAEL, PAULINE. Review of Lisztomania. New Yorker, 51 (24
     November), 171-72.
     Russell lacks a musical sense (as evidenced by the
     rhythm of his editing) and a feel for language. The film
     has a few outrageously funny scenes but remains vague and
     self-indulgent.

484 KASS, CAROLINE. "Movies." Richmond Times Dispatch [Vir-
     ginia] (8 November).
     Lisztomania is "aflash with brilliance," particularly in
     memorable scenes such as the ones in which Wagner vampirizes
     Liszt and becomes the Anti-Christ. [NB, Card 73.]

485 KAUFFMANN, STANLEY. "Tommy." New Republic, 172 (26 April),
     18, 33.
     Russell's style is "ultra-cinematic in the least de-
     manding way," appealing to the adolescent mind.

486 KOSHATKA, EDGAR. "The Travails of Tommy." Philadelphia En-
     quirer (30 March).

1975

> The film is a "modern-day morality play" which also concerns itself with youth's search for meaning and faith. Also includes quotes from Townshend about the work. [NB, Card 26.]

487 KROLL, JACK. "Russellmania." Newsweek, 86 (20 October), 99.
> Russell's "best outrages are vehicles for unique insights." Lisztomania, like some of the TV films and The Music Lovers, is about the Romantic sensibility, which is both glorious and destructive.

488 LAPORTE, CATHERINE [and Ken Russell]. "Ken Russell par Ken Russell." L'Express, No. 1246 (26 May), pp. 11-13.
> Interview dealing, in popular magazine style, with himself and Tommy. In French.

489 LAURSEN, BYRON. "Lisztomania: Insane As Tommy." Willamette Valley Observer [Eugene, Oregon], 1 (28 November), 6b.
> Lisztomania is more effective than Tommy because its vignettes work better--Russell continues to mix "sexual fantasy, outrageous images, cultural history and personal invention without the slightest loss of manic force."

490 _____. "Tommy Barrages the Senses, Woody Mocks the Heavyweights." Willamette Valley Observer [Eugene, Oregon], 1 (11 July), 6b.
> Film is full of "tricks," some of which work and some of which do not. When they fail, "boredom sets in." Tommy is an amusing experience, but it is not to be taken seriously.

491 LEAYMAN, CHARLES D. "Lisztomania." Lancaster Independent Press, 7 (31 October), 8, 10.
> Review disparages criticism such as that of John Simon for condemning a work like Lisztomania out of hand for its biographical distortions without truly understanding it. The film's title is reminiscent of "Beatlemania" and its subject is a similar phenomenon, with a serious side represented by the Fascism of Wagner. It is "funny, exhilarating," but sometimes "confusing." Its "awfulness" stems from the accuracy of its reflection of our times.

492 _____. "Tommy." Lancaster Independent Press, 7 (27 June), 12.
> The original work was not very good, but Russell improves it with his interesting images, creating an "emotional synthesis" of sight and sound. Sometimes, as in the ending shot of Tommy and the sun, the scenes have a power that cannot be explained intellectually. Others, such as the baked-bean sequence, seriously weaken the film.

493   LEFÈVRE, RAYMOND. "Tommy." Cinéma, No. 200 (July/August),
         pp. 143-46.
             Review includes the opera's history as well as a dis-
         cussion of Russell's themes, symbols and style. In French.

494   M., JERRY. "Tommy." Rag [Austin, Texas], 9 (21 April), 13.
             The film is a "euphoric experience" which takes swipes
         at religion, commercialism and the music industry while
         providing a total audiovisual "trip."

495   McCREADIE, MARSHA. "Tommy." Films in Review, 26 (May), 311.
             Russell's approach is right for his subject, producing
         a "kind of awe you wouldn't want to experience again too
         soon."

496   McELFRESH, TOM. "Tommy Among Russell's Best." Cincinnati
         Enquirer (27 March).
             The film is, ironically, "more spare, less sprawling"
         than Russell's other flamboyant movies, when one would
         expect it to be much wilder. [NB, Card 26.]

497   McGILLIGAN, PATRICK. "Too Much Too Little." Take One, 4 (2
         December), 18.
             Lisztomania is "Russell at his utmost," both good and
         bad, but the final result is "an empty gesture."

498   _____, JANET MASLIN [and Ken Russell]. "Ken Russell Faces
         the Music." Take One, 4 (2 December), 16-21.
             Interview discusses Mahler at some length; Tommy, Liszto-
         mania and other films by various directors are also dis-
         cussed. See No. 583.

499   MASLIN, JANET. "Ken Russell Meets Tommy: Gazing at You, I
         Get the Heat." Boston Phoenix, 4 (25 March), Section 2,
         1, 11.
             Russell has a "genius for forging a new style with each
         new film, a style so integral to its subject that the two
         become almost interchangeable." In other works he had a
         starting point--Tchaikovsky's music, Huxley's narrative,
         but the Tommy character is a "cipher." The story is
         brought to life in a series of stunning, evocative images,
         some of which, such as the one in which Frank and Nora
         threaten the child, actually replace the music instead of
         just complementing it.

500   _____. "Lisztless." Boston Phoenix, 4 (4 November), Section
         2, 2, 4.
             Review of Lisztomania.

1975

501 MICHENER, CHARLES. "The New Movie Musicals." Newsweek, 85
(24 March), 56-57, 59.
Tommy is "a phantasmagorical nightmare." The combina-
tion of sound and image is "exhilarating" most of the time.
Russell establishes himself as "the movie musical's answer
to Hieronymus Bosch."

502 MINTON, LYNN. "Tommy." McCall's, 102 (June), 68.
Notice stresses the sadism, violence and grotesqueries
by way of warning parents of impressionable children. Its
overindulgence in "brilliant effects" tends to alienate
all but the already committed.

503 MUNROE, DALE. "Tommy Dazzling Rock Spectacular." Film Bulletin, 44 (April/May), 29.
Review from the "trade" perspective calls film "astonish-
ing" with its excellent production, near-perfect casting,
and "striking" sequences.

504 MURF. "Lisztomania." Variety, 280 (15 October), 26.
Comments on Russell's talent for making an extravagant
film on a small budget. Like most of his films, this one
will please some, displease others.

505 _____. "Tommy." Variety, 278 (12 March), 18.
The "plot betrays its '60s origins," but it makes little
difference; the coherence is best disregarded. The casting of Ann-Margret is "daring" and "effective." The technical aspects are first-rate.

506 NOTH, DOMINIQUE PAUL. Review of Lisztomania. Milwaukee
Journal TV Screen (19 October), p. 8.
Russell needs a strong original source to structure his
talent, as the rhythms of the music in Tommy did. The
Liszt film is dull because lengthy treatment is given to
ideas that should have been fleeting--Wagner as mad doctor,
as vampire, etc. The bombast defeats itself.

507 PAUL, G. A. "Russell's Fun Feast." Films and Filming, 22
(December), 4.
Letter of concern from the Liszt Society prior to the
premiere of Lisztomania.

508 PETERS, JOHN BROD. "Tommy Sacred and Profane." St. Louis
Globe-Democrat (29 March).
The film is "prodigious and prodigal" but loses its
structure near the end. [NB, Card 26.]

509 PHILLIPS, GENE D., JEFF LAFFEL, BERNARD H. GOLDSTEIN. "Ana-
lyzing Ken Russell." New York Times (2 November), Section
2, pp. 15-16.

Letters in response to Davis, No. 446. Phillips ob-
jects to Davis' attempts to categorize Russell's stylistic
development as "straight-line." Laffel defends Russell's
approach to musical biography. Goldstein puts down Davis'
put-down of Russell's savage treatment of Wagner in Lisztomania.

510 POLLACK, JOE. "Rock Opera, Redford, Wayne's Fists--All Fly."
St. Louis Post-Dispatch (28 March).
The viewer of Tommy is "inundated by sound", inhibiting
an otherwise stimulating moviegoing experience. The music
is too brute-strong and repetitious. [NB, Card 26.]

511 POWELL, DILYS. "Clash of Symbols." Sunday Times [London] (30
March), p. 35.
Review of Tommy contrasts other Russell heroes, who are
failures in life, with Tommy, the "image of human triumph"--but finds the image obscured by symbols.

512 _____. "Variations On a Theme." Sunday Times [London] (16
November), p. 37.
There is an excess of vulgarity in Lisztomania, although
some of it works dramatically. Russell makes his point
about the Liszt-Wagner relationship with sometimes beautiful images.

513 POWER, RON. "A Rock Star Reshaped by the Movies." Chicago
Sun Times (17 August), p. 80.
Article on Roger Daltrey which touches on Tommy and
Lisztomania.

514 RAYNS, TONY. "Lisztomania." [BFI] Monthly Film Bulletin, 42
(November), 240-41.
Credits, synopsis, review which calls this Russell's
"first unmitigated catastrophe in years"; it fails because
it lacks structure, and the many film parodies are too wide
of their originals to be successful.

515 REYNOLDS, MICHAEL. "Tortured Trip of Tommy." Berkeley Barb,
No. 506 (25 April), p. 17.
Russell goes for effect at the expense of depth. Some-
times everything comes together well, particularly the
Acid Queen sequence.

516 RICE, SUSAN. Review of Tommy. Media and Methods, 12 (Octo-
ber), 55.
Reads, in its entirety: "Ken Russell's rendering of
The Who's rock opera is loud, really loud."

1975

517   RIPP, JUDITH. "Mahler." Parents' Magazine, 50 (February),
      16.
           Russell's style "finds a perfect subject." The "energy
      and originality" of his work are the result of his risk-
      taking.

518   _____. Review of Tommy. Parents' Magazine, 50 (May), 21.
           "Concreteness is gained at the expense of mystery" in
      the film, and its satire is heavyhanded. There are some
      beautiful scenes and performances, but the movie is "too
      dark" for children to watch.

519   ROBERTS, MARK. "Tommy." Iconoclast [Dallas], 9 (21 March),
      8-9.
           As a narrative, the film is "silly" but engaging. Its
      strengths include the addition of humor to the story, its
      weaknesses, Russell's failure to get uniformly stylized
      performances, and a lack of variety.

520   ROBINS, CYNTHIA. "Director Russell's Tommy Film is Surreal-
      istically Spectacular Project." Columbus Evening Dispatch
      [Ohio] (27 March).
           Russell and Tommy are a "perfect match"; no one but
      Russell, or possibly Kubrick, could have done it justice.
      [NB, Card 26.]

521   ROBINSON, DAVID. "Liszt in the Burlesque Tradition." The
      Times [London] (15 November), p. 10.
           Lisztomania is "execrably silly" but also one of Rus-
      sell's most personal films, reflecting as it does his own
      influences, both cinematically and psychologically; he
      hates Wagner, but also identifies closely with him.

522   _____. Review of Tommy. The Times [London] (27 March), p.
      15.
           "Material and style seem at one" for once. Playing it
      "for all it is worth," Russell produces some "stunning"
      visuals.

523   ROBINSON, KENNETH. "Lisztless." Spectator, 235 (22 Novem-
      ber), 676.
           Flippant plot synopsis, followed by comment that the
      worst thing about Lisztomania is its childishness and
      sometimes dirtiness, but the best thing is that it is
      better than most biopics.

524   ROCKWELL, JOHN. "After Film, Where for Who?" New York Times
      (21 March), p. 29.
           Tommy is Russell's "most convincing effort in several
      years," but his literal approach sometimes bogs down his
      fantasies. Followed by discussion of the soundtrack album
      and the Who.

525 RONAN, MARGARET. "Tommy." Senior Scholastic, 106 (8 May),
     23.
          Russell "somersaults from style to style" but "always
     lands on his feet."

526 ROSENBAUM, JONATHAN. "Tommy." [BFI] Monthly Film Bulletin,
     42 (April), 88.
          Credits, synopsis, review. For once the Russell style
     isn't at odds with his material, but actually helps to
     clarify some of the numbers and to unify them. The best
     sequences visually tend to be the ones containing the best
     songs. The use of the songs to structure the film gives
     it a choppy feeling and a lack of emphasis.

527 RUDIS, AL. "You Could Call Me Franz Lust." Chicago Sun Times
     (19 October), Section 4, pp. 1, 9.
          Background article on Lisztomania based on conversations
     with Roger Daltrey and Rick Wakeman.

528 RUSSELL, CANDICE. "Liszt Film Full of Trash, Freaks." Miami
     Herald (21 November).
          Lisztomania is a "trashy mish-mash" in which costumes
     and sets replace style and content. [NB, Card 73.]

529 SARRIS, ANDREW. "Russell on the Rampage." Village Voice, 20
     (31 March), 69-70.
          Review of Tommy mentions the "double standard" employed
     by some rock critics who object to Russell's approach--
     nobody minded when Disney used pop music for his "doodles,"
     but classics were another matter. Likewise, some critics
     found Russell "too much" for Tchaikovsky and Mahler, but
     "just right" for rock. Tommy's blend of sight and sound
     is "a piece of integrated film" without "malice or smug-
     ness." Discusses the new direction of musical film since
     the sixties, the most significant of which--the Beatles
     films, Performance, etc.--are based on rock. The conven-
     tions are obsolete, and rock's sheer energy is an important
     element to gain audience rapport.

530 SCHICKEL, RICHARD. "Rock Bottom." Time, 106 (20 October),
     61-62.
          The concert scene which opens Lisztomania is "bravura
     irony" and makes its point better than the rest of the
     film, which is "intellectually bankrupt." Russell's is
     a "once interesting sensibility now decayed into vulgarity."
     Followed by short article on Roger Daltrey.

531 SHEAR, DAVID. "Ken Russell and Tommy a Natural Pairing on
     Film." Evening Bulletin [Philadelphia] (27 March).
          Review. [NB, Card 26.]

532   SIMON, JOHN. "Madness, Watchable and Unwatchable." <u>New York</u>,
         8 (27 October), 76-77.
              Russell has a "craving for gaudiness" and an envy of
         and need to belittle his betters. The symbols in <u>Liszto-
         mania</u> are so exaggerated as to be "ridiculous and repel-
         lent."

533   _____. Review of <u>Mahler</u>. <u>Esquire</u>, 83 (April), 58.
              Russell's treatment is "rotten," the film false and
         derivative. It "surpasses in absurdity and hollowness even
         <u>The Music Lovers</u> and <u>The Devils</u>, though in sheer loath-
         someness it may fall just a bit short of that emetic duo."
         Paraphrased in No. 588.

534   SIMS, JUDITH. "Lisztomania." <u>Los Angeles Free Press</u>, 12
         (10 October), 23-24. Reprinted in <u>Rochester Patriot</u> [New
         York], 3 (23 October), 9.
              Russell's seeming indifference to Liszt "has freed him
         to make a vivid, astounding movie." Daltrey isn't actor
         enough to give Liszt any depth, although the director is
         more interested in Wagner anyway.

535   SINEUX, MICHEL. "<u>Tommy</u>." <u>Positif</u>, No. 171-72 (July/August),
         pp. 107-108.
              Convoluted discussion of the failure of this "calami-
         tous" film. In French.

536   SISKEL, GENE [and Ken Russell]. "The Big Scene Grabber Hits
         Again in the Movie <u>Tommy</u>." <u>Chicago Tribune</u> (25 March),
         Section 3, p. 2.
              Russell discusses composers and their music. Siskel
         remarks on one of Russell's main problems as a commercial
         director: "an outlandish scene grabs the public's atten-
         tion, and the film is lost for those who can't see past
         their outrage."

537   _____. "<u>Lisztomania</u>: a Lot of Garish Imagery by a Former
         Filmmaker." <u>Chicago Tribune</u> (30 October), Section 3,
         p. 4.
              Russell liberated the biopic, but he is now going too
         far. This film is better at attacking Wagner, because of
         the strong visuals, than it is at portraying Liszt. The
         director's "considerable" talent has lately been squandered.

*538   SMITH, HOWARD and BRIAN VAN DER HORST. "See Me, Feel Me,
         Hype Me." <u>Village Voice</u>, (10 February), p. 18.
              [Cited in Gomez, No. 578, p. 223.]

539   SMITH, LIZ. "The What?" <u>Cosmopolitan</u>, 178 (June), 14.
              <u>Tommy</u> is fascinating but dated. It is also a bit be-
         wildering because of the constant transitions from realistic
         to mystic to symbolic.

540   SOPHEIA, DALE. Review of Tommy. Primo Times [Bloomington, Indiana], No. 24 (2 September), p. 13.

541   SPENCER, DENNIS. "Tommy Unreal Movie; Also Unusual, to Say Least." Birmingham News [Alabama] (27 May).
      The plot's vagaries are annoying. [NB, Card 37.]

542   STABINER, KAREN. "See Me, Feel Me, Botch Me, Steal Me." Santa Barbara News and Review, 4 (11 July), 19.
      Tommy suffers from "sensory bloat" and is "bits and pieces of disjointed stimulation." The plot is constantly undermined by the production numbers, and Russell's technique with actors makes most performances "fairly grand and fairly empty."

543   STARK, SUSAN. "Pinball Wizard Film Registers a Noisy Tilt." Detroit Free Press (28 March).
      Tommy is witless and vulgar, although its cast gives it wide audience appeal. [NB, Card 26.]

544   STERRITT, DAVID. "Tommy--England's Rock Opera." Christian Science Monitor [Eastern edition], 67 (1 May), 26.
      The film is energetic, visually exciting, and unconventional in its "view of life and art"--but it is also distasteful, crude, and artistically inconsistent.

*545   _____ [and Ken Russell]. "Whole Film is 'One Flash' In His Mind." Christian Science Monitor (2 June), p. 27.
      Interview discusses Tommy. [Cited in Gomez, No. 578, p. 220.]

546   STJERNE, HARALD. "Tommy." Chaplin, 17: 225-26.
      Review. In Swedish.

547   STOOP, NORMA McLAIN. Review of Lisztomania. After Dark, 8 (December), 101, 103, 106.
      Much of the film is "outrageously funny," but the satire is "heavyhanded and banal" near the end. Enough truth lies beneath the distortions and nightmarish fantasies to give at least some understanding of Liszt.

548   _____. Review of Mahler. After Dark, 7 (March).
      The film is "bizarre and beautiful," and captures the "Zeitgeist which Mahler fought in his art and conformed to in his life."

549   _____. Review of Tommy. After Dark, 8 (May), 34.
      The film is "a cinematic turning point" in which image and music merge and interchange.

1975

550   TAYLOR, FRANCES. "Ken Russell Expands Reality for Controversy."
      Star-Ledger [Newark, New Jersey] (8 June).
            Compares the excesses of Tommy with those of other Rus-
      sell films. The theme of the commercialization of religion
      and other topics are discussed in excerpts from an inter-
      view with Russell. [NB, Card 37.]

551   TAYLOR, ROBERT. "Is Ken Russell as Crazy as His Movies?"
      Oakland Tribune [California] (24 February).
            Review of Mahler describes some of the film's wilder
      scenes, and includes excerpts from an interview with
      Georgina Hale. [NB, Card 20.]

552   _____. "Tommy: Delirious Savagery." Oakland Tribune [Cali-
      fornia] (25 April).
            The viewer feels "raped" by the movie's visual style
      and noise level. Performances of the individual actors
      are "overpowered" by the film. [NB, Card 37.]

553   TESSIER, MAX. "Tommy." Écran, No. 38 (July/August), pp.
      52-53.
            Review, credits. In French.

554   THOMAS, BARBARA. "Lisztomania Is Adventure Into Absurd."
      Atlanta Journal (5 November).
            Film is "outrageous, stylistically inventive." [NB,
      Card 73.]

555   _____. "Unlikely Cast Directed Well." Atlanta Journal (1
      April).
            "The fun of watching a Ken Russell film is the visual
      shock, stretched to the point of ridicule and finally to
      hilarity." However, this may not be quite the right treat-
      ment for Tommy and its "sensitivity." [NB, Card 25.]

556   THOMAS, J. N. "Russell's Mahler a Serious Film." Berkeley
      Barb, No. 507 (2 May), p. 17.
            The film's exploration of the Mahler-Alma relationship
      is poignant and evocative, an amalgam of fact, feeling and
      Russell's personal reaction. Through his striking images
      he can communicate a wealth of information in a few frames.

557   TOWNSHEND, PETE. "Who's Tommy." Films and Filming, 21 (June),
      18-21.
            Discusses the creation and recording of Tommy. The film
      is mentioned in passing and there are several stills from
      it.

558   TUMBLESTON, ROBBIE. "Tommy." Great Speckled Bird [Atlanta],
      8 (3 April), 16.

Film is "in a class by itself" as it wrings "every
nuance, irony, and satiric bit of popular culture" from
the opera. It is a dreamlike puzzle with an interesting
cast.

559   VINCENT, MAL. "Lisztomania a Suspense of Nonsense." Virgin-
      ian-Pilot [Norfolk] (10 November).
          Using several examples from the film, discusses the
      "silly overproduction" and purposeless dream sequences.
      [NB, Card 73.]

560   WHITE, RON. "Tommy: A Panoply of Insane Visions." Express-
      News [San Antonio, Texas] (6 April).
          The film is "a work of genius" which explores and re-
      defines creativity as it attacks commercialism. Discusses
      the particular appropriateness of the pinball metaphor, and
      Russell's use of his actors to portray specific types.
      [NB, Card 26.]

561   WHITMAN, MARK. "Soundtrack Records." Films Illustrated, 5
      (December), 156.
          Review of Lisztomania album.

562   WILSON, DAVID. "Tommy." Sight and Sound, 44 (Summer),
      192-93.
          Film is uneven, but the parts in which Russell is in
      tune with his material are "dazzling." Discusses his
      style in this context, concluding that he needs "a special
      relationship with his material" to fully display his talent.

563   WINE, BILL and JIM BUGNO. "Tommy--Deaf, Dumb and Blah."
      Drummer [Philadelphia], No. 341 (25 March), pp. 12-13.
          Wine: The film never "touches" the audience. The mix-
      ture of "hallucinatory phantasmagoria and sophomoric ex-
      cessiveness" is merely "dizzying." Bugno: The film clari-
      fies the opera's intent somewhat, but it still seems ab-
      surd.

564   WITKOWSKI, DENNIS. "Tommy Flashy But Weak." Fifth Estate
      [Detroit], 10 (3 April), 10. Reprinted in Rochester
      Patriot [New York], 3 (23 April), 13.
          The film fails to satisfy, looking cheap and gaudy
      and hinting at a "heavy message" that doesn't exist.

565   WUNTCH, PHILIP. "Russell's Tommy in Song." Dallas Morning
      News (21 March).
          Film is "70% inspiration and 30% indulgence," but the
      inspiration is so good that the indulgence is forgiven.
      [NB, Card 26.]

1976

566   ALLEN, TOM, S.C. "Programming Mahler." <u>America</u>, 134 (8 May),
      415-17.
          Russell is "one of today's most blinded, egotistical,
      self-destructive directors." He can be bad (<u>The Devils</u>,
      <u>Lisztomania</u>); he can leave good moments in mediocre films
      (<u>Tommy</u>, <u>The Music Lovers</u>); or he can be "astoundingly
      forceful (<u>Women in Love</u>, the TV films). <u>Mahler</u> is both
      "the zenith and the nadir of his career." Some of the
      transfigurations of music to image are perceptive and
      sensitive, yet the composer's life is simplified. Russell,
      whose style has been evolving "from a base of romantic
      naturalism towards a psychic surrealism," has revolution-
      ized the biopic; his work will last despite his excess.
      In <u>Mahler</u>, his obvious love for the music helps him to
      create some beautiful images to counteract the "embar-
      rassing juvenalia" of his more exotic sequences.

567   ANON. "Russell, Ken." In <u>Current Biography</u>. Edited by
      Charles H. Moritz. New York: H. W. Wilson Co., pp.
      369-72.
          Fairly thorough synopsis of the highlights of Russell's
      life, as well as comments on his films and their acceptance,
      or lack of it, by public and press.

568   ATKINS, THOMAS R., ed. <u>Ken Russell</u>. New York: Monarch
      Press, 132 pp.
          Varied, interesting profusely illustrated anthology
      contains: 1) Atkins--a funny screenplay for a biopic on
      Russell, using his own methods; 2) Gene D. Phillips--
      article on the amateur films <u>Peepshow</u> and <u>Amelia and the</u>
      <u>Angel</u>; 3) John Baxter--article on the TV films; 4) Jack
      Fisher--analysis of <u>Women in Love</u>, <u>The Music Lovers</u>, and
      <u>The Devils</u> (reprint of No. 241); 5) Joseph A. Gomez--study
      of Russell's methods of adaptation in <u>Savage Messiah</u> and
      <u>Tommy</u>; 6) Excerpts from <u>Mahler</u> and <u>Tommy</u> screenplays; 7)
      Short biography; 8) Filmography; 9) Selective bibliography.

569   BOWMAN, JON. "Film Fantasy Tribute to Romantic Composer."
      <u>Albuquerque Journal</u> (14 March).
          Review of <u>Mahler</u> says that critical condemnation of
      Russell's films is exaggerated; critics are intolerant of
      his individuality and the non-narrative quality of his
      screenplays. [<u>NB</u>, Card 23.]

570   BUNDOLINI, JASMINE. "Devilish Delight." <u>Films and Filming</u>,
      22 (January), 4.
          Reader's letter, with an appreciation of Russell's pre-
      vious work and critique of <u>Lisztomania</u> which finds the
      director's premise of Wagner-as-musical-vampire erroneous.
      <u>See</u> No. 581.

571   CAIN, SCOTT. "Even Tacky Russell Worth Price of Ticket."
        Atlanta Journal (7 July).
            Russell is the most tacky, unforgiveable, imaginative
        and striking film biographer. The scenes of excess in
        Mahler are "top-flight," the rest is mild by his standards.
        The performances are larger-than-life and excellent. [NB,
        Card 52.]

572   CARON-LOWINS, EVELYNE. "Lisztomania." Positif, No. 180
        (April), pp. 72-73.
            The film combines several genres--musical comedy, horror,
        historical--with a look at the nature of good and evil.
        In French.

573   COCKS, JAY. "Hardly Classical." Time, 107 (17 May), 74.
            Mahler is "discombobulated, flatulent," full of turmoil,
        both Mahler's and that which Russell adds. It has neither
        Tommy's wit nor The Devils' "full-tilt craziness," but it
        has "stunning flashes of beauty" among the foolishness.

574   COOK, PAGE. "Mahler." Films in Review, 27 (June), 377-78.
            The "stunning" film contains both "manic hyperbole"
        and "devastating insights."

575   EDER, RICHARD. "Ken Russell's Mahler." New York Times (5
        April), p. 45.
            Russell's cinematic "dreams" tell more about the dream-
        er than their subjects. He doesn't let his films exist
        outside himself. The most excessive scenes in Mahler bury
        the film's "real qualities" and the real insight into
        Mahler's character.

576   ELLEY, DEREK. "Lisztomania and The Loves of Liszt." Films
        and Filming, 22 (January), 31-33.
            Russell's choice of the pop-star idiom is fitting, but
        his real advantage is the way in which he takes his idea
        beyond all bounds. As usual, the fantasies are just barely
        based on fact and reveal more of Russell than of his sub-
        ject.

577   GILLIATT, PENELOPE. "Genius, Genia, Genium, Ho Hum." New
        Yorker, 52 (26 April), 119-21.
            Comments on silly moments in other musical biopics
        lead to comments on Russell and his interpretation of
        Mahler. His films are "tenth-rate, overblown porno-
        graphic fantasies." The film puts more than necessary
        emphasis on Mahler's alleged guilt at his conversion
        from Judaism to Christianity.

1976

578   GOMEZ, JOSEPH A.   Ken Russell: The Adaptor as Creator.
       London: Frederick Muller Limited, 223 pp.
            Complex, scholarly book, interestingly illustrated,
       contains: a foreword by Russell; an introduction, deal-
       ing with film adaptation in general and Russell's methods
       in particular; "From Amateur Films to Isadora Duncan: Rus-
       sell's approach to Biographical Films and the Development
       of a Personal Style"; "Dante's Inferno, Song of Summer,
       and The Dance of the Seven Veils: Three Approaches to
       Adaptation"; "Women in Love: Novel into Film"; "The Music
       Lovers: The Importance of Metaphor"; "The Devils--Rus-
       sell's Major Achievement: Sources"; "The Devils--Rus-
       sell's Major Achievement: The Film"; "Savage Messiah:
       Truth Through Exaggeration"; "Mahler: Further Experiments
       with Metaphor and Personal Vision"; "Tommy and Lisztomania:
       The Beat Goes On"; "Conclusions"; Filmography and bibliog-
       raphy.

579   GOW, GORDON [and Ann-Margret]. "Something to Offer." Films
       and Filming, 22 (January), 12-16.
            Interview includes comments on the filming of Tommy,
       particularly the difficulties of filming the baked-bean
       sequence.

580   GREENFIELD, PIERRE. "Dirty Dogs, Dirty Devils and Dirty
       Harry." Velvet Light Trap, No. 16 (Fall), pp. 34-37.
            Despite critical damnation, Straw Dogs, Dirty Harry
       and The Devils are "very moral" films which "force the
       spectator to question his own nature and outlook." Straw
       Dogs demonstrates, with both its lead character and the
       action's effect on the viewer, the ease with which violence
       can become pleasurable. Dirty Harry presents a basically
       mean character as admirable; he commits an illegal but
       sympathetic act of violence and the audience is left to
       decide whether he has acted properly. The viewer's identi-
       fication with the "reprehensible" aspects of Grandier's
       character in The Devils makes him recognize his own pecca-
       dilloes and, through the calculating depiction of the
       events at Loudun, engages his unemotional, unsentimental
       moral indignation.

581   JONES, P. S. RODERICK. "Roll On Russell." Films and Filming,
       22 (February), 4.
            Reader's letter, refutation of No. 570.

582   KOPKIND, ANDREW. "Music Mit Schlag." Real Paper [Boston],
       5 (16 June), 29.
            Mahler is a bit "too much"--too much gooey romanticism,
       too much heated fantasy. Russell "sometimes succeeds as the
       intellectual's Disney," making as much sense of great men's
       neuroses "as Disney did with Snow White's." When he begins
       to take himself seriously, the fun ends.

583 MANNS, TORSTEN, JANET MASLIN and PATRICK McGILLIGAN. "Kom-
     ponister På Hjärnan." Chaplin, 18: 58-62.
         Synopsis of Lisztomania, historical background on Liszt
     and Wagner, short critique of film. Swedish translation
     of the Take One interview, No. 498.

584 MERINOFF, LINDA [and Oliver Reed]. "Penthouse Interview:
     Oliver Reed." Penthouse, 7 (January), 92-96, 116, 124,
     164.
         Long, entertaining interview with frequent references
     to the actor's work for Russell.

585 MORAN, DAVID. "Mauler?" Boston Phoenix, 5 (22 June), Sec-
     tion 2, p. 3.
         In Mahler, Russell shows his "feeble understanding of
     human nature" and understands the facts of Mahler's life
     but not its psychology. The film can be interesting for
     the patient viewer, but "Russell's concessions to his bad
     taste always trip up any possibilities of his imagination."

586 ROSENBAUM, DAVID. "Second Sight." Boston Phoenix, 5 (14
     September), Section 2, p. 3.
         Russell's "rococo" style often alienates his audience.
     In the case of The Devils, it overbalances and ultimately
     destroys the film with excess and the "desire to shock
     and disgust."

587 SHERLOCK, M. G. "The Devils." Films Illustrated, 5 (Jan-
     uary), 191.
         Combined plot synopsis and review which concludes that
     its comparison with Straw Dogs and A Clockwork Orange
     is unfair: the violence in it is neither gratuitous, as
     in the former, nor "lyricised and glorified" as in the
     latter.

588 SIMON, JOHN. Notice of Mahler. New York, 9 (10 May), 65.
         Paraphrases earlier review, No. 533.

589 TESSIER, MAX. "Lisztomania." Écran, No. 45 (March), pp.
     68-69.
         Russell totally rejects historical facts and the methods
     of making historical films for a movie that is all metaphor
     and fantasy. In French.

590 WINSTEN, ARCHER. "Mahler: Complex Tale of the Composer's
     Life." New York Post (5 April).
         The viewer would benefit from prior knowledge of
     Mahler, for clarity's sake and so that the "free associ-
     ations" are more meaningful. [NB, Card 23.]

1977

591   ANON. "NureyeValentino." <u>Playboy</u>, 24 (October), 171-73.
      Photo preview.

592   BLAND, ALEXANDER. "Tamerlane of the Performing Arts."
      <u>Horizon</u>, 20 (September), 28-34.
         Article on Rudolf Nureyev discusses his dancing and his
      acting in <u>Valentino</u>; several photos of Nureyev from the
      film and otherwise.

593   GOW, GORDON [and Glenda Jackson]. "One-Take Jackson." <u>Films
      and Filming</u>, 23 (January), 12-18.
         Jackson discusses working with Russell, saying that he
      provides an atmosphere in which she can develop acting
      ideas, without being very specific in his directing. He
      always knows exactly how he is going to film his "big"
      scenes, while much less certain about intimate ones.

594   MEWBORN, BRANT. "<u>Valentino</u>: Ken Russell's Tango Hustle."
      <u>After Dark</u>, 10 (October), 46-53.
         Profusely illustrated preview speculates that, given
      his various raw materials, Russell should be able to
      fantasize to his heart's content.

595   _____. "Valentino: Rudi Plays Rudolph." <u>After Dark</u>, 9
      (March), 74-75.
         Photo preview.

596   SISKEL, GENE [and Rudolf Nureyev]. "Nureyev: Stepping Into
      the Role of Valentino." <u>Chicago Tribune</u> (2 October), Sec-
      tion 6, pp. 1-4.
         Interview deals with the character of Valentino as
      perceived by Nureyev and by Russell (the film seems
      "ambiguous" perhaps because of the difference in their
      perceptions) and with dance.

Other Film Work and Writings

AMATEUR FILMS (Director)

1956

*597   PEEPSHOW.

*598   KNIGHTS ON BIKES (unfinished).

1957

*599   AMELIA AND THE ANGEL.

1958

*600   LOURDES.

TELEVISION FILMS (Director)

[These films, varying in size from about ten minutes to feature film length, were all made for the BBC Monitor series. I am grateful to John Baxter's An Appalling Talent: Ken Russell (London: Michael Joseph, 1973) for the information in this list.]

1959

*601   POET'S LONDON (with John Betjeman).
        Shown 1 March.

*602   GORDON JACOB.
        Shown 29 March.

*603   GUITAR CRAZE.
          Shown 7 June.   Repeated 24 July 1960.

*604   VARIATIONS ON A MECHANICAL THEME (mechanical musical in-
          struments).
          Shown 27 September.

*605   UNTITLED FILM (artists Robert McBryde and Robert Colquhoun).
          Shown 25 October.   McBryde section repeated 8 May 1966.

*606   PORTRAIT OF A GOON (Spike Milligan).
          Shown 16 December.

                              1960

*607   MARIE RAMBERT REMEMBERS.
          Shown 17 January.

*608   ARCHITECTURE OF ENTERTAINMENT (John Betjeman).
          Shown 28 February.   Repeated 15 December 1964.

*609   CRANKS AT WORK   (John Cranko).
          Shown 24 April.

*610   THE MINERS' PICNIC   (brass bands).
          Shown 3 July.

*611   SHELAGH DELANEY'S SALFORD.
          Shown 25 September.

*612   A HOUSE IN BAYSWATER.
          Shown 14 December.   Repeated 25 June 1968.

*613   THE LIGHT FANTASTIC (dancing in England).
          Shown 18 December.

                              1961

*614   OLD BATTERSEA HOUSE (Pre-Raphaelite museum).
          Shown 4 June.

*615   PORTRAIT OF A SOVIET COMPOSER (Sergei Prokofiev).
          Shown 18 June.   Repeated 6 August 1962.

*616   LONDON MOODS.
          Shown 5 November.

*617   ANTONIO GAUDI.
          Shown 3 December.

1962

*618   POP GOES THE EASEL (Pop artists).
        Shown 25 March.

*619   PRESERVATION MAN (Bruce Lacey).
        Shown 20 May.

*620   MR. CHESHER'S TRACTION ENGINES.
        Shown 1 July.

*621   LOTTE LENYA SINGS KURT WEILL (co-director Humphrey Burton).
        Shown 10 September.   Repeated 19 August 1964.

*622   ELGAR.
        Shown 11 November.   Repeated 16 May 1963, 26 June 1966,
        16 July 1968.

1963

*623   WATCH THE BIRDIE (David Hurn).
        Shown 9 June.   Repeated 15 July 1964.

1964

*624   LONELY SHORE.
        Shown 14 January.

*625   BARTOK.
        Shown 24 May.   Repeated 9 July 1968.

*626   THE DOTTY WORLD OF JAMES LLOYD.
        Shown 5 July.   Repeated 2 July 1968.

*627   DIARY OF A NOBODY.
        Shown 12 December.

1965

*628   THE DEBUSSY FILM.
        Shown 18 May.   Repeated 12 June 1966.

*629   ALWAYS ON SUNDAY (Henri Rousseau).
        Shown 29 June.   Repeated 2 July 1968, 1 June 1969.

1966

*630   DON'T SHOOT THE COMPOSER (George Delerue).
          Shown 29 January.

*631   ISADORA DUNCAN, THE BIGGEST DANCER IN THE WORLD.
          Shown 22 September. Repeated 26 March 1967, 19 March 1969.

1967

632   DANTE'S INFERNO (Dante Gabriel Rossetti).
          Shown 22 December.

1968

*633   SONG OF SUMMER (Frederick Delius).
          Shown 15 September.

1970

*634   THE DANCE OF THE SEVEN VEILS (Richard Strauss).
          Shown 15 February.

1971

635   Discussion between Russell, Alexander Walker and George
          Melly. Film Night--Confrontation, BBC-TV. Telecast 28
          February. [Cited in Gomez, No. 578, p. 219.]

1973

636   "Ken Russell Interviewed by Colin Wilson." Camera Three,
          CBS-TV. Telecast in two parts, 23 and 30 September.
          [Cited in Gomez, No. 578, p. 220.]

COMMERCIALS

*637   Twenty or so advertisements for commercial television in
          the mid-sixties. Include Black Beauty chocolates, Hor-
          licks baked beans, Galaxy chocolate bars. Seen in Britain.

WRITINGS

*638   "Ideas for Films." Film, No. 19 (January/February), pp. 13-15.
        [Cited in MacCann, Richard Dyer and Edward S. Perry. The New Film Index. New York: E. P. Dutton and Company, Inc., 1975, p. 311.]

1972

*639   "Ken Russell Writes on Raising Kane." Films and Filming, 18 (May), 16.
        [Cited in Schuster, Mel, comp. Motion Picture Directors: A Bibliography of Magazine and Periodical Articles, 1900-1972. Metuchen, New Jersey: The Scarecrow Press, Inc., 1973, p. 333.]

1974

640   "Personal Choice 1974." Listener, 92 (19 and 26 December), 819.
        Russell is one of several prominent people who enumerate their favorite moments of 1974 British television; most of his have to do with musicians.

Archival Sources

There are no known collections specifically on Russell; however, the following institutions have material on him and/or his work.

641   MARGARET HERRICK LIBRARY
       Academy of Motion Picture Arts and Sciences
       8949 Wilshire Blvd.
       Beverly Hills, California 90211
       Phone: (213) 278-8990
           Contains biographical files on Russell, as well as production files, which include clippings, reviews, and stills, on all his feature films.

642   NATIONAL FILM ARCHIVE
       81 Dean Street
       London, W1V 6AA
       England
       Phone: 01-437-4355
           Holdings are exhaustive in the area of books on film and television, and of film periodicals and ephemera. Clipping files are kept on film personalities, but as of 1973, the file on Russell seems to have been quite superficial. The archive also has prints of at least the major TV films done by Russell.

643   LIBRARY OF CONGRESS
       10 First Street S.E.
       Washington, D.C. 20540
       Phone: (202) 426-5840
           Has 35mm reference prints of all Russell's feature films. They may be viewed at the library, free of charge, by appointment.

Film Distributors

644   COLUMBIA PICTURES, 300 S. Colgems Square, Burbank, California, (213) 843-6000; 711 Fifth Avenue, New York, New York, (212) 751-4000.

        Lisztomania (Columbia-Warner)
        Tommy

645   CONTEMPORARY/McGRAW-HILL FILMS (16mm) Princeton-Hightstown Rd., Hightstown, New Jersey 08520, (609) 448-1700; 828 Custer Avenue, Evanston, Illinois 60202, (312) 869-5010; 1714 Stockton Street, San Francisco, California 94133, (415) 362-3115.

        Amelia and the Angel (16mm)

646   FILMS INCORPORATED, 733 Green Bay Road, Wilmette, Illinois 60091, (312) 256-6600; 5589 New Peachtree Road, Atlanta, Georgia 30341, (404) 451-7445; Suite No. 423, Oak Cliff Bank Tower, Dallas, Texas, (214) 941-4236; 5625 Hollywood Boulevard, Hollywood, California 90028, (213) 466-5481.

        The Boy Friend (16mm)
        Savage Messiah (16mm)

647   METRO-GOLDWYN-MAYER, 10202 W. Washington Boulevard, Culver City, California, (213) 870-3311; 1350 Avenue of the Americas, New York, New York, (212) 977-3400.

        The Boy Friend
        Savage Messiah

648   SWANK MOTION PICTURES, INC., 393 Front Street, Hempstead, New
      York 11556, (516) 538-6500; 5200 W. Kennedy Boulevard,
      Tampa, Florida 32609, (813) 870-0500; 4111 Director's Row,
      Houston, Texas 77092, (713) 683-8222; 7926 Jones Branch
      Drive, McLean, Virginia 22101, (703) 821-1040; 1200 Roose-
      velt Road, Glen Ellyn, Illinois 60137, (312) 629-9004; 220
      Forbes Road, Braintree, Massachusetts 02184, (617) 848-8300.

          Tommy (16mm)

649   TIME-LIFE FILMS, 43 W. 16th Street, New York, New York 10011,
      (212) 691-2930.

          Dante's Inferno (16mm)

650   UNITED ARTISTS, 1041 N. Formosa, Los Angeles, California,
      (213) 851-1234; 727 Seventh Avenue, New York, New York
      10019, (212) 575-3000.

          Billion Dollar Brain
          The Music Lovers
          Valentino
          Women in Love

651   UNITED ARTISTS 16, 729 Seventh Avenue, New York, New York
      10019, (212) 575-4715.

          Billion Dollar Brain (16mm)
          The Music Lovers (16mm)
          Women in Love (16mm)

652   VISUAL PROGRAMME SYSTEMS, 21 Great Titchfield Street, London,
      W1P 7AD, England, 01-580-6201.

          Mahler

653   WARNER BROTHERS, Warner Brothers/7 Arts Films, 4000 Warner
      Boulevard, Burbank, California 91522, (213) 843-6000;
      Warner Brothers Distributing Corp. 75 Rockefeller Plaza,
      New York, New York, (212) 484-8000.

          The Devils
          French Dressing (Warner-Pathé)

654   WARNER BROTHERS (16mm), Non-Theatrical Division, 4000 Warner
Boulevard, Burbank, California 91522, (213) 841-1500.

The Devils (16mm)
Lisztomania (16mm)

Author Index

Film Title Index